TWISTED TALES

My Life as a Mongolian Contortionist

OTGO WALLER

BALBOA.
PRESS

A DIVISION OF HAY HOUSE

Balboa Press books may be ordered through booksellers or by contacting:

Balboa Press
A Division of Hay House
1663 Liberty Drive
Bloomington, IN 47403
www.balboapress.com
1 (877) 407-4847

Print information available on the last page.

ISBN: 978-1-5043-7861-1 (sc)
ISBN: 978-1-5043-7863-5 (hc)
ISBN: 978-1-5043-7862-8 (e)

Library of Congress Control Number: 2017905676

Balboa Press rev. date: 04/20/2017

FOREWORD

When I was a little girl, whenever I could, I would lie in the grass and stare up into the beautiful Mongolian sky. I would study the clouds as they traced across their big blue backdrop. Their shapes, the way they moved, the direction in which they traveled—all of these qualities would send my mind racing. I would become mesmerized. As curious as I was back then (and still am, if truth be known), I always wanted to know, above all else, where this cloud would travel once it had passed beyond my sight.

"Where will this one go?" I would ask myself. "I don't know. Maybe somewhere in Russia. Or *China*. Or maybe somewhere in Europe." Of course, as a young girl, I didn't have a clue where America was, so the possibility that a cloud might travel so far was never even a consideration.

Another thought I would often have when enjoying my favorite childhood pastime was that no matter what time of day and no matter what condition the sky, at any given moment, someone somewhere in the world would be looking up at the sky, just as I was. And at any given moment, perhaps they were thinking the exact same things that I was thinking. Eventually—whether it would be a few minutes, a few hours, or a few days—this other person might even see the very same clouds I was seeing as well. They would experience the same shapes, the same movements, the same cloudy paths.

As I write this book, I keep those two wistful thoughts from my childhood in mind. Like a cloud, we all have our own unique journeys to undertake. And like a cloud, with its relationship to the grand playground that is the sky, we are all connected.

My mother always taught me that you have to be honest in everything you do. "When you are honest," she used to tell me, "nothing holds you back. So always be honest and do the right thing."

Well, if I am to be honest in this account of my life, the first thing I must come clean about is that I didn't always want to be a contortionist. In fact, there is a part of me that still aspires to be something else. The truth is that, deep down, I always wanted to be a journalist. It's that curiosity that drives me. Just as I was always curious to know everything about every cloud I saw, I have always been curious to know everything about everyone I meet. I have always had a gift for talking to people. It has never mattered whether they were difficult to talk to, never mattered what age, class, religion, skin color, or sex they were. I could get to know them. My curiosity and genuine desire to know them would always allow them to open up to me.

But the funny thing about curiosity is that it is often a one-way street. The most curious people are often hesitant to share anything personal about themselves. I have always been that way. I could drive my family and friends up the wall with all of my questions, but whenever the questions were turned on me, I would close myself off. I was quick to learn, but never to share. Until now.

Whenever I'm asked why I wanted to write this book in the first place, the answer is always the same. In my life, I have experienced many difficult times. I have known great pain. What I have learned above all over the years is that pain is a constant and never-ending struggle, but hope is its greatest antidote. And so I hope to reach anyone, even if it's just one person, who might be experiencing similarly difficult times or pain, and I hope to show them that they're not alone in their struggle. I hope to show them that there was at least one young Mongolian girl who wanted to give up at many times in her life, a girl who often thought that the pain was just too much to bear. I hope to show them that, like the clouds we see almost every day, they are not alone.

Life can deal a difficult lot to anyone, no matter their race, color, or creed. Life can often overwhelm, but the answer is never to let it. The most important thing is to fight back against the difficult times, to work hard toward a dream. The central story of my life is that as often as I fell down and felt sorry for myself, I always got up and kept going. Even in the darkest times, I always prayed to God, always hoped that things would get better for me and my family.

And family is an important thing—perhaps the most important thing. Since I was a little girl staring at clouds, I have taken care of myself, but never at the expense of others. My family has always come first. In turn, they have helped me to get through those difficult times. They have helped me to heal.

My quality of life has greatly improved since I was a budding contortionist in Mongolia, but I'm still working. I still struggle. Hard work and determination have carried me here to America, and I have no doubt that they will continue to carry me. I am so thankful for what I have.

The names of some of the people who appear in this book have been changed. Though many of them hurt me physically, mentally, and emotionally—though several of them even abused me sexually—I choose to respect their privacy and dignity. Also, I should point out that much of the first chapter of this book is a secondhand account, as told to me by my sister, Noyo. Apart from these minor considerations, this is the true and honest story of my life.

Today is Thursday, April 6, 2011. The time is 5:50 p.m. Until this moment, I have held my pain inside. Until this moment, I had no desire to ever share my stories. But I am ready now.

Otgontsetseg Waller

CHAPTER 1

My oldest sister, Noyo, was pregnant with her first child. Labor pains came to her on the same day and time that one of the great Communist leaders of Eastern Europe was due to visit our homeland of Mongolia. My family found everyone at the hospital to be unusually busy and excited. The doctors and nurses darted in all directions, some of them helping Noyo.

"Your daughter is going to be a very lucky girl," one of them told my sister. "Her timing is impeccable."

While the nurse would prove prophetic on the sex of Noyo's unborn child, her soothsaying on the condition of her luck would prove shoddy. Even before my little niece reached her first birthday, she took ill and passed away.

My family was devastated. My sister, mother, and father even visited a monk. In the Buddhist tradition, when someone dies, the family of the deceased visits a monk, who performs a special service called *Altan Xairtsag Neekh* (Open the Golden Box). The monk is spiritually connected to the departed soul and can tell at the time of death what she was thinking and what, if anything, she would like for the family to do in regard to a funeral.

I am told that when the monk opened my niece's golden box, he said that she was a very special and lucky little girl, and that, if she had lived, she would have had anything in the world she desired.

My mother and father turned to one another, tears lining their eyes as they embraced. My sister held her steady gaze on the monk, wanting to know more.

"Zuurdaar!" the monk said, startling my family. I was told that his expression became grim and wary, the candlelight rendering his wrinkled face into an ominous dance. "Please don't bury her."

"What would you have us do?" Noyo asked.

"If you leave her on the highest mountain, and if you pray and offer religious merit, she may return to your family."

"Return?" my father asked skeptically.

"Yes," the monk said, bowing low. "She will return to you in a new form, as a child yet to be born."

So my father took my niece and wrapped her in a blanket. He carried her alone onto our highest and most sacred mountain, the Bogd Uul. There he left her on the windswept peak, returning down the mountain as a man weary from journey and ravaged in spirit.

A month passed. My family prayed.

One night, my mother dreamed that her granddaughter, alone on the mountain, had risen and taken to wandering the countryside. Between her delicate hands, she held a candle. She wandered as though lost. Then, in the dream, she came upon our *ger* at the base of the mountain. She found my mother and ran to her. The moment my mother stooped to embrace her grandchild, she woke from the dream.

Two months passed. My family prayed.

There came a time when my mother didn't feel so well. She had been gaining weight for several weeks. She felt constantly tired. The first morning that she was sick in the yard, she knew that she was pregnant. This came as quite a shock to her, as my mother was forty-two years old at the time.

When she told my father and my sister of the news, she did so as a woman utterly beside herself with confusion. Dad and Noyo were happy, of course, and encouraged my mother to keep the baby.

"But I'm forty-two," she said. "Women my age can't have a baby! What will the neighbors say?"

"Don't worry about what the others will think," Father said.

"Yeah, who cares?" Noyo said.

Together they convinced my mother that this unexpected miracle was worth maintaining.

Three more months passed. Then a fourth. Mother didn't leave the house much, owing partly to embarrassment and partly to her fear that any sudden movement might lead to complications at her age. Dad and Noyo took care of most of the chores and errands, such as going to market for groceries.

Two months passed. I was brought into this world.

There I was, the youngest of six children, the first born in a hospital. My mother, Butedsuren Natsag, could not have been a more wary or loving mother. My father, Adiya Tsagaan, was the proudest father on our whole nomadic street. Norjinsuren ("Noyo" for short) was the oldest of my siblings and the most doting, due to the monk's prophesy. Tsogtmagnai ("Tsogoo" for short) came next. Then Bayraa, Enkhtsetseg ("Enkhee"), Enkhnaran ("Naraa"), and finally, Otgontsetseg ("Otgo"), your humble narrator.

When I was born, my family lived in the shadow of the holy Bogd Uul, near the Mongolian capital city of Ulaanbaatar, a name that means "Red Hero." This wasn't always the city's name. It was once called Ikh Khuree (also known as "Great Camp"), but the newly formed Mongolian People's Republic Party made the switch to Ulaanbaatar.

Our neighborhood, Zaican Tolgoi, Ulaanbaatar, was once a nomadic tent city, with houses that looked like wigwams. The townspeople would move their makeshift homes from pasture to pasture, allowing their animals to feed. Their homes were sturdy and wooden, warm in the winter and cool in the summer, and roomy but utterly absent of privacy.

By 1924, the town had come under Russian influence, and the

Mongolian government became a puppet state of Lenin and Stalin. As the twentieth century progressed, Chinese and Russian workers constructed a number of permanent buildings. By the time I was born, the downtown of our capital city was lined with many small concrete or steel buildings, all them square and bland, save for one: the Mongolian State Circus, which was a beautiful domed structure constructed of blue glass.

The Bogd Uul was a holy mountain. Hundreds of years prior to my birth, the land upon the mountain had been set aside as a nature preserve. Any man caught hunting or poaching from the land was punished. We are a people much connected to the earth. Every natural element and every life is sacred.

And so, when I was born, my family lived at the foot of a holy place and at the mouth of a drab and typically Socialist city. Our ger, the traditional Mongolian tent home, was large and sturdy, and our yard was surrounded on all sides by tall wooden fences designed to promote privacy. We didn't have much: three small beds, one large trunk to keep our clothes and other things, a table, and a fireplace. Every home on our street was nearly identical. The roads were shabby, constructed of dirt and lined with many potholes.

My siblings were much older than me, so I confess that I had a fairly lonely childhood. The two youngest of my sisters, Enkhee and Naraa, still lived in the house with my parents when I was born. The other three had already moved on to their own homes, however. I was close with Enkhee and Naraa—close enough even to fight with Naraa about clothes and shoes.

My father was a war hero. He fought for our country in the war in 1939 as well as in 1945, garnering a number of medals along the way. My mother was a part-time hospital maintenance staff member. She was also a highly religious woman. She would pray every morning, and every night she would take me to Gandan Kheed, the biggest and only Buddhist temple that the Communists didn't destroy. I have the purest memories of my mother kneeling in the Temple of Gandan Kheed, feeding and praying to the many pigeons of the temple. She was a woman of deep passion and love.

My parents worked hard to provide for us, but, with six children to feed, money was always tight. Yes, we were poor children living in a poor house. Many nights, we ate whatever we had—which was often things as odd as cow head or sheep intestines.

Whenever I recall our hand-to-mouth upbringing, I often think of one kparticular story of my father. It was autumn, and Dad had taken ill. But sick as he was, he knew that if he didn't do something drastic—and soon—we would have to begin choosing which nights of the week we would eat.

So, with a great and chill wind howling down the Bogd Uul, Father stalked into the woods to gather *samar*—nuts. He left at dawn, promising to return home by dusk.

The day came and went, and Father never returned. He didn't come back that night. By the following afternoon, we were all a little worried.

"Maybe the nuts were picked over, and your father had to climb," Mom reasoned.

For a time, this stilled our concern. But when two more days passed and Father was still missing, we grew altogether wracked with worry. We kept our spirits high, encouraging each other that our father would soon return, but we all suspected that something awful had happened.

Dismayed though we were about Father's absence, we tried to pass the time in the way that we always passed time. Each morning, Enkhee and Naraa would walk to school, and I would run after them, crying because I wanted to go with them.

"Go home!" they would yell.

"You're still too young!"

"Maybe next year."

I would trudge home alone to find that Mother had left for work at the hospital. These were different times, and this was a different place. Daycare for children wasn't something that most people even considered. And when you were poor, your mother had to work just like your father. So at six years old, I would stay home by myself. I would pass the lonely hours of the day by sitting on the wooden fence that surrounded our yard. I would sing to myself and watch the people of the neighborhood in all their constant toiling.

It was never frightening, being alone and so young, but it was always frustrating. Whenever the children would play in the streets or in their yards, I would want to play with them, but I knew I couldn't. I would be left only to watch—watch and hum from my wooden perch surrounding my tent garrison of a house.

The reason I took to watching other people at such a young age was because it was really the only thing I could do. We didn't have any toys for me to play with. Not until I was ten years old did I receive my first toy: a little ball. My lack of toys and our always patched and hand-mended clothes served as a constant embarrassment to me and my sisters in our youth. Whenever someone came to our house, I would hide under the bed, ashamed about the many different colors of patches my mother had sewed into my only pair of pants.

In the evening, the girls would return from school, a magical place in my mind. They would greet me dully, and we would go inside to begin our nightly chores. From the time I could walk, Mom taught me many things about how to care for a home. I learned how and had to help with cleaning the house, cooking, washing my clothes, and taking care of my own needs in almost every respect. If I did a poor job of washing, she would make me do it again. Idle time was rare.

"If you have nothing to do," Mom would say, "then you're wasting precious time."

Sometime later every evening, Mom would return home, and on good days, we would eat meat. On bad days—like the days when Father went missing in the mountain—we would eat doughy bread, if anything at all.

The fifth day of Dad's absence passed in harrowing silence. One of the most I vivid memories of my childhood is that of my mother sitting in the corner of our broad and open house, saying nothing, staring off into space. It was entirely unlike Mother to sit still for long, but I seem to remember her wallowing through the evening hours in this way until it was time for her to turn down our beds.

By the sixth day, Mom could do little but cry.

"He only wanted to make some extra money for his family," Mom pled, her sight turned to the heavens. "He only wanted to provide for us, to feed us, please God. And now we don't know what happened to him."

We were all seated around the table near the stove, our arms crossed in front of us, lumped in the place where our dinner bowls would rest whenever there was money. Mom sobbed now into her hands, her shoulders heaving.

"Maybe he got lost," Enkhee said, shrugging.

Naraa picked at her teeth with her tiniest finger. "Or maybe some wild animal ate him."

Mom erupted into a wild bawl. She pulled me—her nearest child—to her chest, squeezing me to the point of breathlessness. For a time, she rocked in her seat as she held me to her. She sobbed. Her breathing stuttered. She quivered. And then, all at once, her crying ceased. I looked up at Mom, expecting to see her looking a mess. But instead, what I saw was a woman totally at peace, a woman who had pulled herself together for the sake of her children.

"He will come," she said, as certain as I had ever heard her sound. Her left eye boggled in her head, green and mismatched to her right, which was brown.

Mom had a fake left eye. At night, she would take it out and keep it in a glass jar filled with water. The story goes that, sometime before I was born, Mom and Dad were leaving the countryside, Mom being seven and a half months pregnant with my older brother, Tsogoo, and in need of medical attention. For several weeks, the village had been passing around a terrible pinkeye infection. Mom contracted one of the worst cases. Pregnancy is not the ideal time for infection when you live in Mongolia, so Father decided to take his wife to the city to get help. It took them many days of traveling from our village to Ulaanbaatar.

En route, Mom's infection got worse. There was a point when she couldn't even open her eyes, they were so swollen.

By the time they reached the city, Mom was in wretched condition. They would have a bit of luck, however, because a pair of doctors from Russia happened to be visiting the hospital in Ulaanbaatar at the time. They advised that, given Mom's condition, it would be best for the mother and baby if they removed the eye. Right after the surgery, Mom gave birth to a baby boy.

So Mom was left with a baby and no left eye. Dad bartered with the Russian doctors for a glass eye, but unfortunately, they didn't have any on hand, so it wasn't until they arrived back home in Russia that they could actually complete the order. After the order finally went through, Mom received a bright, shiny, green eye. She plugged it into her skull, and there it had swirled in contrast to her natural brown eye ever since.

"He will come," she repeated.

For as long as I can remember, I have loved the story of Buddha. Organized religion was generally frowned upon in Mongolia in those days, but the stories nevertheless passed from ear to ear, the relics remaining hidden among the populace. I remember many vivid pictures of Buddha, their colors mesmerizing. I was drawn to them from quite a young age.

I guess my mother saw something of the zealot in me because she agreed to allow me to go to my Aunt Amaa's house to learn of the Buddha and his ways. Aunt Amaa was Dad's youngest sister, and she was a skinny woman of middle age. I remember her short, dark hair.

Amaa was remarkably outspoken in her religiousness, given the political climate. And she practiced what she preached, caring for her two daughters and four grandchildren all in the same poor home. Her only possessions of value were her Buddha statues, which she would keep in a locked chest above her fireplace.

It was Amaa who would first teach me the ritualistic way to pray. We would kneel before her biggest Buddha statue and offer candy and money. She would always end the prayer by settling into a throw pillow to tell me stories of the Buddha. One afternoon, while my sisters were away at school, Aunt Amaa even let me clean her shrine and polish her lovely statues. I took great care and time with the task, dusting and shining every inch of her shrine with a delicate woolen cloth.

"Oh my, Otgo," she said as she stood over my handiwork. "You did a wonderful job."

I beamed.

"You didn't change one thing," Aunt Amaa said, placing her hands on her hips. "Everything's in its right place."

I blushed and pawed at the edge of her shrine, examining my own glorious work.

"You can clean my Buddhas any time you like!"

On exactly the seventh day after Father had first left into the mountain, I heard, from far away, someone calling our names. It was night, the air crisp, the dust of the roads deadened by the late afternoon's rain.

"Enkhee!" came the voice. "Naraa!"

Naraa brightened up, her brown eyes shimmering in the candlelight. Without a word, she ran in the direction of the voice. I followed as quickly as my little legs could carry me. I was six and a half years old, and I remember this day as if it were yesterday.

"Did you hear?" I hollered as we passed Enkhee. "Did you hear?"

I didn't wait for my sister's response. Instead, I tore through the front gate, chasing Naraa toward the dark horizon.

"Dad!" Naraa howled. She reached him first, barreling into his arms.

Father laughed heartily as I joined my sister. He set down the bag he carried to take me into his arms as well. He held me tight, his chest heaving through his infectious laughter. I looked down from my father's embrace and saw the burlap sack he had been carrying. It was filled to overflowing with nuts.

When we returned to our ger, we entered silently. Mom turned only at the sound of the clacking front door.

"Oh dear God!" she said, holding her hand over her mouth.

Father smiled.

"What happened to you?" Mom barked.

I examined my father's appearance as if for the first time. He looked terrible. Downtrodden. He was unshaven and wraith-skinny. His shoes had been ripped nearly in half at the soles, and he had done what he could to repair them with tree bark and twine. At the corner of his left shoe, I could see his dirty toes exposed to the elements.

Dad dropped the bag of nuts on the floor, a handful of them skittering out of the bag. Mom ran to him and wrapped her arms around him. Naraa and Enkhee went to the bag, each filling their hands with delicious nuts.

"How did you do this?" Mother asked, noticing the bag for the first time. "You have brought so many."

Father smiled as he took a seat at the table. He moved slower, I noticed.

His bones appeared creaky, like a much older man's. It was as if he had aged many years in only a few days. Enkhee took a seat next to him, spilling the contents of her shirt on the table. Naraa sat across from father. She picked up a nut and began picking at its shell. I sat next to father, who sat at the head of the table, and did the same. Mom sat at the other end of the table. We all gathered around for a story.

"I went to the usual grove," Father said, "but there just weren't enough nuts. So I went farther into the mountain. I came through a pass, traveled through a heavy thicket of trees, through a spiny wood, and finally came to a clearing. There, I found more of these beautiful nuts than I have ever seen in one place. I filled my bag to overflowing, and I filled my pockets too." Reflexively, Dad looked down at his pants, which were torn and wrinkled and improbably muddy. "But I had to eat those that I kept in my pockets as I made my way home."

"You walked for three days into the mountain?" Mom asked incredulously.

Father shook his head. "Only one day. It was difficult traveling to the clearing, but it is not far."

"Then why were you gone so long?" Our mother's tone was sharp and terse, angry enough to cause us all to freeze and turn to stare at Father.

He shrugged. "I got lost."

Mom seethed for a moment, but then her face softened and the color returned to her cheeks. "But you're home now."

"I found my way back," Father said. Then he smiled, patting Enkhee on the arm as she reached for another nut. "I *had* to. I had to find my way back for my children."

The next day, Father took ill. We cleaned the nuts. I can remember the smell of the nuts even now—a piney smell, an earthen one. When we had filled several large buckets with the freshly cleaned nuts, Enkhee and Naraa went to the street to sell them. If we were lucky, they would come home with enough money to go to the grocery store on the edge of town. Perhaps it would feed us for several days. Perhaps we would have enough money to buy Father some medicine. This was our life.

CHAPTER 2

It was rare for a home to have a television, but I was lucky enough to have a neighbor friend who had one. The family with the TV would always point the television toward an opening in their ger so it could be seen from the yard. Depending on whom you believe, this tradition was designed either to accommodate watching a program from the relative coolness of the outdoors or to broadcast to the entire neighborhood that one particular family on the block was fortunate enough to have a TV.

I was over at my friend's house one day, and they had the television blaring in the usual way. None of us were paying it much attention as my friends and I performed cartwheels. But then I noticed something out of the corner of my eye. Through the flickering black and white light, I saw a young, slender woman in a white bikini. She lay on the surface of a small, round table and began twisting her body into tight ringlets. The way she moved, the way she bent herself, it was like she was more snake than woman. It was mesmerizing. I found myself in awe.

"That's that famous contortionist!" my friend's mother said. "Kids, come look."

My friends quit playing and joined me beside the TV. They were all in awe of the talented woman, who had now walked her ankles behind her shoulders, folding her body and moving into a chin-stand.

"What's her name again?" my friend's mother asked. "Some famous lady?"

Her husband stepped out of the ger, holding a cup of green tea, his traditional costume rippling in the breeze. "Oh, that's Norovsambuu," he said. "The contortionist."

"Norovsambuu," I whispered. In that moment, all the usual little girl dreams faded from me. I no longer wanted to be a journalist or radio anchor. I wanted to be just like Norovsambuu.

When the sun began to set and our mother called us home from the yard, I ran straight to our ger and began to bend myself. At first, I tried small things—pulling my ankle behind my head. And I always did it in as much privacy as I could manage, which was very little. I would contort myself on the bed because there was a hanging sheet at the foot of the bed. I would contort myself outside in the yard while the others prepared for bed. I would contort myself inside the ger while the others were at school and work. I knew that I had discovered a new passion, but I did not want my mother to find out. She was a traditional and hardworking woman. From what I could guess, she would never want her daughter chasing such silly dreams.

My secrecy only lasted a few weeks, but by the time I was first found out, I had already learned to bend myself in half. Mom caught me in a particularly compelling knot. I was tied up in such a way that it took me a moment to unfurl when I first heard her frightened scream.

"What in the world are you doing?" she barked as I settled back on my haunches.

"I don't know," I said, my eyes already brimming with tears.

"Well, don't do it again!"

I nodded and went back to my chores.

Of course, this was a lie. I would spend every private moment for the next year trying to bend myself into a coil. I kept working on the few things I remembered seeing on the television program with the famous contortionist. The way Norovsambuu performed the act on TV had been so graceful. Her movements were fluid. Mine were clunky and strained. I could bend my limbs in many strange ways, but it was never a lovely thing to watch. Where Norovsambuu was a taut ballerina, I was a clumsy lump.

Around the time I finally came of age for school, Mom caught me for a second time. This time she wasn't confused. She was only furious. She yelled at me until her faced turned red, and when I was properly crying, she took out her remaining anger on Noyo, who was visiting for the weekend with her husband.

"I leave you in charge and you let her do this!" she hollered.

"No, Mom," Noyo insisted.

I would have leapt to her defense, explaining that Noyo was, in fact, telling the truth, but I was too busy bawling in the corner.

"You knew she was doing this, and you did nothing to stop her!"

Noyo's hands balled into fists in the way they always did when she was defying Mother. "You're wrong!"

"That's it!" Mom shouted. "Otgo, if I catch you doing this again, you won't be going to school!"

This broke me. Where I was sobbing before, I had now broken into a deep wail.

"Look at this," Noyo said, casting a hand in my direction. "You see what you're doing to her?"

Mom's hard shell cracked only for a moment.

"There's no use in forbidding your daughter's dreams," Noyo insisted, looking as if the point struck home a little too closely for her liking. "It doesn't matter how much you want her to stop, she's going to do this anyway."

My sobbing slowed at the words. When I looked at Mother, her shoulders slumped. She turned for the door, shaking her head defiantly. But she said no more. I looked then at Noyo in awed appreciation. My eldest sister, the woman who gave birth to my spiritual precedent, had stood up for me as if I were her own daughter. I loved her deeply in that moment, for she had come to my aid.

In the weeks that followed, Mother still didn't seem to approve of my contortionist habit, but she never forbade me again. Things were much easier after that.

———❧———

Noyo was a tall, slender girl with dark hair and big, brilliant eyes. Whenever she visited, it seemed to put us all at ease. Something about her carriage, or about the optimist's sense she carried at all times, brightened our ger like firelight. On her next visit, she came straight up to me upon entering our door.

"Otgo," she said with an inquisitive smile, "are you still doing your contortion?"

I looked warily at Mother, who frowned and turned her head away. I nodded.

Noyo took a step back, gesturing to the floor. "Show me something."

I showed her all that I had taught myself. It wasn't much, but what I could do, I could do quite well.

"Wow!" she said when I had finished. "You're getting good."

I smiled at my big sister. A quick glance at Mother made my smile broaden. Though the rest of her face remained locked in its look of disgust, the light in her eyes was that of maternal pride.

The two women then retreated to the yard, murmuring to each other in hushed tones, Noyo obviously excited and Mom clearly miffed. When they returned, Noyo was smiling. Mother was not.

"Put on some clean clothes," Noyo said impishly.

"Are we going somewhere?"

My big sister giggled.

We took a bus two stops from our neighborhood into the downtown area of Ulaanbaatar. From the bus, we made the short walk in the sun two blocks down concrete sidewalks and between concrete buildings. Noyo led the way with light strides. I skipped through my confused excitement. Mom trudged behind.

"Aren't you going to tell me?" I asked Noyo.

My sister giggled. "I keep telling you, it's a surprise."

Our journey ended at one of the biggest buildings I had ever seen. It was gray and constructed of two floors. We passed through several square rooms full of tall, angular people before we found our way into a giant room at the end of the building. The ceiling rose up high overhead.

My eyes widened at the many sights. There were grown men and women in the room, but mostly children. The children were dressed in tight, colorful clothing. Some of them hopped around, doing rudimentary gymnastics. Others juggled. Still, others performed contortions.

Noyo knelt in front of me and told me to wait for her. I nodded, and she left me standing with Mother. Mom's eyes were as wide as mine, her green eye swirling in the socket. It calmed me to know that she was as mystified as I was.

I watched as my eldest sister went up to an older man dressed in black pants. The man's hair grayed at the temples, but apart from that, he was in excellent shape. His face was handsome, though accented with wrinkles, and his body was hard and svelte.

He spoke to my sister for a time, occasionally casting appraising glances in my direction. He appeared delighted to make Noyo's acquaintance and ready to watch me perform. When they finished speaking, he waved to me.

"Come on!" he called, his voice as soft as his demeanor.

Sheepishly, I walked toward them, trying to take comfort in Noyo's prideful grin. I stood before the kindly man, unable to look him in the eye.

"Come then, girl," the man said encouragingly. "Let's see what you can do."

I blushed. With my toe, I traced a small circle over the floor. I stood with my hands behind my back, feeling petrified by shyness.

"It's okay, Otgo," Noyo urged. "Just show the man what you showed me."

Quivering from nerves, I rolled to the floor and began to bend myself. Though it was essentially just this man, my sister, mother, and me—surrounded, of course, by many dozens of practicing children—I could not have felt more under the microscope. I had never before felt so uncomfortable. But I believed in my abilities as a contortionist and did my best. When I finished, I stood demurely before the man in black.

"Good," he said. "You can start tomorrow."

Startled, my eyes darted to Noyo, whose fists shook at the air in delighted thanks. I ran to her, and she embraced me.

"Does this mean I get to train here?" I asked her.

I could feel Noyo's nod atop my head. When she let me go, she was beaming. I turned to thank the man, but he was already gone, disappearing into the crowd of budding performers. I felt a hand on my shoulder. My mother. To my surprise, she had a smile on her face. To my greater surprise, she now looked overwhelmed with pride. I melted. Never was there a child happier in all the world. Warmed by my mother's approval, I stared into the crowd. The smell of chalk and sweat reached my nostrils—the first time I would experience the aroma that best solidified my life.

"That was good," Mother said.

At my carefree young age, I still was not entirely sure what my mother was talking about. All I knew was that the man in black had liked my bending. Little did I know that his approval would launch for me a contorted life.

Back at home, Noyo was beside herself as she reviewed the details of our meeting with the man from the circus. Father was silent but obviously proud. Mother still seemed very much on the fence. There was no hiding Naraa and Enkhee's excitement. I had learned on the bus ride home that I had been selected to train as a contortionist. This was one of the highest cultural honors that a child could be bestowed at the time. I still wasn't sure how I had managed such luck, but I did know that my eldest sister was instrumental—and so I stared lovingly at Noyo for several days after.

"Now you'll have to take her to practice tomorrow," Noyo said. "She shouldn't take the bus alone."

I looked to Mother, who was already shaking her head, looking exhausted. Everything about her posture and expression suggested that she would refuse to drive me anywhere, but to my surprise, she agreed with a sigh. "Of course I'll take you, Otgo. But you have to do your best."

I nodded with grand vigor.

"If you don't do your best, my mission in this life will be incomplete."

My heart surged with determination. "I will make you proud of me, Mom."

So that is how I started my life as a contortionist. When I got home from school each day, Mom would go along with me to practice. We would have to take the bus. Since I was just over eight years old, I didn't have to pay for a ticket, but Mom did, and this was no small expense for my family. Dad was quite sick at the time and had to remain in bed, which meant he couldn't work. By then, Mom was retired. So our only income was Mom and Dad's pension, which amounted to very little. Somehow, Mom managed to juggle all our expenses. Sometimes this meant cutting down on our food. Sometimes this meant we would have to walk to my practices.

The buses in Mongolia were more like giant VW buses: boxy, rickety, and lined near the top with smaller windows. We called the bus the "auto bus," because that's what the Russians called it, and in the school, we were required to learn to speak Russian. There were not many cars, and those that could be found were most often government cars.

The gym where I trained was stripped down. Only the essentials for training could be found there. The floor was wooden, and there was very little equipment to aid in our training. The children were nicer than I would have guessed going in. Everyone helped each other.

My coach turned out to be the man in black with whom Noyo had spoken. His name was Khishegt, and he proved far kinder than his often terse expression suggested. He taught me a great deal in a very short time. Only a few months after I had begun at his school, I was prepared to perform my first show in Terelj, a small tourist town near the capital of Ulaanbaatar. I was nine years old.

The show would feature a full cast of acrobats, jugglers, and contortionists, all of them students from our school. My coach would serve as director and producer of the show, and through his guidance, we would

OTGO WALLER

be slated to perform for a full hour. My segment would run a particularly trying four and a half minutes, and I would have to do it solo.

I shivered backstage for the first thirty minutes or so of the show. My nerves had never been more overwhelming. By the time it was my turn to take the stage, I could scarcely think, let alone process all that was happening. I could see that my table had been set up for me at the center of the stage. The table was oval shaped and smooth. Mercifully, I could barely see the audience, given that the floodlights drowned out my vision.

My routine would be simple. I did plenty of bending and almost no strength work. Being as remarkably flexible as I was, I could contort my limbs like a veteran, but being as new as I was to the game, I wasn't yet strong enough to perform some of the more dramatic positions that would later define my career.

Still nervous, I bent and flexed on the table, the sound of traditional and soft instrumentation filling my ears. I had heard this music many times before, as Mongolian contortionists tended to use it.

What I remember with great detail is the moment that my show ended. I slid from my table and took a bow to a soft roar of applause. A fiery heat reached my cheeks as I bowed a second time. My limbs began to tingle. My lips began to part in a joy I could hardly contain. The rush of applause. This would be my first taste, and there is nothing like it.

I bounded from the stage on the balls of my bare feet. There, just beyond the curtain, I plowed into the waiting arms of my coach, who clapped me on both shoulders and looked down on me with almost fatherly pride.

"You did a wonderful job," he said, grinning broadly.

I giggled and swooned. He clapped me on the shoulders again, his attention turning to the next act taking the stage. I hopped away, giddy. My modesty didn't allow me to revel for too long in my success, however, and I tried to remind myself that I was still young and learning. It would be a long time before I could become the next Norovsambuu, I told myself. There would be many months and years of training before I could even graze her level of greatness. For now, I only take pride in the fact that I hadn't fallen. For everything else, there would be room to improve.

In Mongolia, a circus show is traditionally followed by an informal and wildly entertaining encounter with the members of the audience. The full cast comes out from backstage and the audience gets the opportunity to meet them. From here, for a good two hours, the audience and cast mingle, dance, and carry on in jolly fashion. This was my first experience with this sort of thing, so even the lighthearted nature of the post-show event made me nervous. I don't recall much about what happened, but I do know that I was one of the shyer members of the cast, preferring to keep to the corners, blushing more than I danced.

Time moved quickly in those days. I would go to school, train, and return home to sleep. We would hold performances here and there in many small venues. Mom kept taking me to practice, and I kept improving.

One day, Khishegt called us together outside his office. His eyes flickered with an excited light, dancing as he spoke.

"We have been invited to perform at the Mongolian State Circus!" he said, emphasizing his excitement with his thick, rough hands.

We all cheered. It was quite an honor to perform at the state circus. When compared to the crowds we were used to playing for, the audience would be enormous. We would be carrying out our acts in front of professional performers as well. It would require a great deal of training.

CHAPTER 3

The Mongolian State Circus is a cylindrical building of glass and concrete, crowned by a jagged dome. The dome's surface darts in several geometric angles, all of them coming to points at the eaves of the more modest base of the building. The roof is painted a lovely blue that matches the sky almost perfectly. The round base of the building is lined with many windows, the natural light shining in from all sides.

Attached to the domed performing wing of the building is another structure, this one square and two stories high. While the cylinder contains the performance arena—the seating holding a thousand people—the second building houses the performers' dressing rooms and the administrators' offices. There was a pair of training rooms, one of them dedicated solely to contortionists. Near the back of this structure, the circus offered a giant stable in which to house the ponies, monkeys, camels, bears, and other animals on showcase.

At my young age, when I first took a tour of the State Circus, I found myself most in awe of the dressing rooms. I longed to be a performer, after all, and the private showers, plush couches, and vanity mirror all appealed to me quite deeply. In all, the facilities were second to none. I knew even then that this was why Mongolian circus performers were so often world-renowned: they had the best facilities in which to train and rehearse.

Shortly after being led through the building—the other children and I being entirely slack-jawed—we were all asked to set up and perform our rehearsals. We had been practicing for nearly a month, so the routines had become rather mechanical. For my contortion act, I was to perform with two other girls. I would be in the middle, with the others flanking me. Given the excitement of the day, and of being introduced to this grand and historical place, we rehearsed with more vigor than usual. I bent myself with a grace and ease that I had never experienced before.

As we rehearsed, I began to notice that two women about Noyo's age had come into the practice room to watch. At first, they scanned the room of aspiring performers casually, but after a time, they seemed to train on us. With every new position I took, they would speak to one another in excited tones. It was clear that they were talking about us—and in looking at my performance partners, I could see that they saw it, too—but none of us could quite tell whether they were speaking in flattering or derisive terms.

I remember little about my first performance at the State Circus, only the rehearsal. It was the first time in my young life that I had been exposed to true professionals, and to my heart's great joy, they appeared to approve.

I sat in my favorite spot on the practice room floor. My mother waited in the hallway. The rest of the contortionists in my group sat cross-legged in a loose circle at the center of the gym. Khishegt paced before us, his hands gesturing wildly again.

"I can hardly believe it," he said, "but I guess good news comes in bunches." He looked to Tuya, the female coach of our group, who smiled. "Children, we will be visited soon by the famous contortionist Norovsambuu."

Everyone squealed with delight—everyone but me. I was too busy reeling in shock to make any sound. Norovsambuu. The woman who had inspired me to become a contortionist in the first place.

"We have decided that one of you can go to perform for Norovsambuu, who has agreed to give the selected performer her advice."

My heart raced. Only one act would get to meet with my hero. And then my heart sank. There was no way that my act would be granted the opportunity.

"By the end of practice today," Khishegt said excitedly, "I will let you know which act has been chosen."

The other girls cheered. In that moment, I sized them all up. There were many great performers in our troop. In my mind, there was simply no way I would ever be selected for the fateful meeting.

Despite my doubts, I went through the motions at practice with grave determination. I stretched with catlike grace. I held myself up on two hands. The coaches seemed pleased.

When practice ended, I ran to fetch my mother. I felt warm from the practice, but not tired.

"Otgo," came a voice.

I turned to see Khishegt. My coach looked far more eager than normal. He fired a nervous glance at my mother and then extended his hand to me. "Can I see you in my office?"

My heart began to pound. Such was my denial at the possibility that I might be chosen to perform for Norovsambuu that my first instinct was to assume that I was in trouble. "What did I do?" I asked my coach.

Khishegt laughed and led me into his office. It was a tiny but remarkably clean space. My coach slid around his desk with surprising grace, settling into his small wooden desk chair in a fluster. He motioned for me to take a seat in the only other chair in the room.

"Otgo," he said with a smile, "I have chosen you to be the one to perform for Norovsambuu."

I fell back in my chair, pressing a hand to my heart. I couldn't believe it. My lips curled at the corners. It was like a dream come true. I thanked my coach and ran to my mother.

"That's wonderful!" she said, sounding happy but looking suddenly alarmed.

"What is it?" I asked her, concern spreading across my face.

"What are you going to wear?"

I laughed. It was true that I didn't have any nice clothes—certainly not any clothing befitting a nervous performer for the queen of contortionism—but I knew that Mother would figure something out. She always did.

As we waited for the bus, I could hardly handle being in my own skin, let alone standing still. I was too excited to be contained. I considered asking Mom if we could skip the bus so I could run home, but she looked tired, so I waited, bending at the knees and clapping every now and then. Finally, the bus came, and we made the short ride home.

The moment the bus's door opened, I sprang ahead of Mother and bolted from the stop, through the gate, and into the yard. I found Dad in the house, lounging on his bed as he often did in those days.

"Father!" I called.

He stirred, startled from sleep.

"I'm going to perform for Norovsambuu!"

Father furrowed his brow. He still seemed to be passing between the sleeping and waking world.

I giggled. "You know … the contortionist?"

Dad's face came to light. He rolled over on his side, propping himself up on an elbow. "*That* Norovsambuu?"

I nodded, grinning broadly.

He leaned forward and kissed me on the forehead.

Several days passed, and my excitement about meeting a national icon never wavered. Mom fretted for hours on end about what in the world I was going to wear. Then, one morning, she presented me with a brand new set of white tights.

I looked at her, aghast. "Mom, how can we afford these?"

"Just promise me you'll wear this on the day of your performance," she said with a sad smile.

"Of course I will, but—"

"We can manage," she interrupted. "Just please don't wear them before. I don't want you to get them dirty."

I was so happy that I ran to Naraa to show off my new gift. Of course, I wanted nothing more than to try it on.

"Let's see how you look in it!" Naraa squealed.

"Don't get it dirty!" Mom yelled.

I sulked, slumping onto my bed. Frustrated, I tossed the tights into the small suitcase where I kept the rest of my clothes. I spent the rest of the night trying to concentrate on the evening routine: dinner, chores, preparing for sleep. But every chance I got, I would pull out my new tights, test their stretch, smell them, admire them, and then put them back.

That night, I couldn't sleep for thinking about my brand new tights. It would be the first non-used set that I would ever wear, and the anticipation was killing me.

It was all I could do to sit through school the next day. By the time I got home, I could no longer stand it. I knew I wasn't supposed to wear my new tights, but I took them out of my suitcase, gave them one more sniff, and pulled them on. They felt so smooth and comfortable, like they were made just for me. I sat on the bed and kicked my legs a little, feeling the stretch at the hamstrings. I reveled in their newness, their comfort, their dedication to me.

I knew I had to practice in them. Mom was not yet home from her daily errands. I had beaten Naraa and Enkhee home from school. Father was at the doctor. I had the house to myself. So I lay down on my bed and practiced a new pose. With my hand pressed to the floor, I cocked at the elbow and pushed myself into a handstand. With both legs in the air, I began to feel myself shake at the base. I righted my center of gravity by kicking out with my right leg—not my best pose, but this would do.

Then something went wrong. My arms shook. I lost my balance all at once and tumbled hard, my legs catching against the corner of the bed. I felt the fall and heard the tear. The left leg of my tights had caught on the metal frame of my bed, tearing along the seam. I stood to find that I had ruined my new outfit. Mother would kill me.

What will I tell her? I thought. Fear crept over me. My face felt flush, my hands numb.

And then I knew what I had to do. I had to hide it. I stripped out of my new tights and buried them back in my suitcase.

—◦◦◦—

When the big day came, my mother seemed a ball joy. All smiles, she bounded into the ger and told me to put on my tights.

"Aren't you excited to wear your new outfit?" she asked.

I hung my head, dejected.

"Don't just stand there," Mom said. "Go put your tights on. I want to see how they look."

I remained rooted to the floor.

"Why are you just standing there?"

At the words, I finally turned, my head still hanging. I swept over to my suitcase and reluctantly fetched the damaged tights. When I returned, I handed them over to Mom. She frowned in her disappointed way. Her hands worked busily over the fabric. In short order, she found the tear.

"When did this happen?"

A lump formed in my throat. "Wednesday."

Mom's face brightened to red. "Then why didn't you tell me about it on Wednesday?"

I looked down at my feet, trying not to cry.

Father chose that moment to join us. "What's taking so long? We're going to be late."

Mom flashed me with a furious glare. The look softened when she held up the tights to her husband, who groaned. Without another word, my mother went to the corner of the ger opposite the fireplace, where she rummaged through the chest. In time, she produced her sewing supplies, and with lightning speed, re-stitched my tights.

She returned the tights to me with a grumble. "Now hurry up and put your clothes on."

I took the tights and scampered away to the other end of the ger.

"Your father's right. We're going to be late."

All the way to our destination, I cried. Mom tried to quiet me, but I knew it was wrong what I had done. When we reached the venue where we would meet Norovsambuu, the event had already started. I was upset about my tights and stressed about being late.

By the time my act was called, I was not at all worried about my performance—not because my nerves had faded, but because I was too worried about what I was wearing. My performance was acceptable, but I wasn't quite myself. I felt self-conscious throughout, felt like I was preening and moving too slowly to be considered graceful. I had let my mother down.

I lowered myself from my last pose, took a quick and disgusted bow, and stormed out of the small room. Coach Khishegt was waiting in the hall for me. He looked happy. Proud.

"You were wonderful," he said, his voice carrying much higher than usual.

"I was okay," I said.

"No, you were more than okay."

I nearly laughed, I was so confused. If only my coach could have gotten inside my head during the performance; he would have seen that I had never been so lifeless onstage.

"Norovsambuu was interested in you," he said.

I lost my breath.

"She wants to meet with you personally."

I bit my lip. "What?"

"After the event," he said, nodding excitedly. "Just don't be too overwhelmed. She just wants to talk to you."

The day's anguish was suddenly replaced by an overwhelming wave of excitement. It was all I could do to keep from leaping out of my skin, let alone my refurbished tights.

"After the event," my coach said. He took my shoulders in both hands, smiled, squeezed, and moved past, returning to the room.

When the event had ended, Coach Khishegt found me waiting with my mother outside the small room in which we had held our performance. I had told her the news, and she was obviously a little beside herself. Mom seemed hesitant to let me go with my coach alone, but when he mentioned that Norovsambuu wanted to see me only, Mom backed away. Feeling giddy and nauseated at the same time, I followed Khishegt back into the performance room.

There sat Norovsambuu, every bit as simple in appearance as she had looked on TV. She was not terribly tall, but not overly short. She was, however, quite thin. Her dark skin and shoulder-length black hair accentuated her rounded cheekbones. The low-cropped bangs framed her dark eyes well. She carried a serious, almost skeptical expression upon my entrance. As I took my seat and began waiting for her to speak, I saw that the expression never really faded. This was a hardened woman, a woman quite used to the injustices of the world.

I stared up at Norovsambuu. Unsmiling, Norovsambuu stared down at me. She asked me to stand. I stood. She asked me to turn around. I turned. She told me to sit. I sat.

"Tomorrow," she said, "bring your mother with you to the State Circus. I'll be waiting."

I nodded from the moment she finished speaking to the moment she shooed me out the door. In my five minutes before Norovsambuu, I hadn't said a word. This was not unusual, necessarily. In Mongolian tradition, children never speak to adults unless spoken to. But on this occasion, things had been different. Norovsambuu didn't ask me any questions. She didn't seem to want to know anything about me except for how I looked. And when I obeyed—perhaps *because* I obeyed—I was awarded with a trip to the State Circus, a trip with cryptic purpose.

The next day, Mother and I went to the State Circus. Norovsambuu met us in the lobby and took us to her room. It was a vast but simple dressing room, with its own shower and a small beige sofa and two chairs, one of them soft and upholstered and the other short and wooden. Norovsambuu took a seat on the sofa, crossing her legs and looking up at us.

"Show me what you can do," she said. "And I mean *everything*."

I felt suddenly naked. I might have come dressed for practice, but I had not planned on performing. When I looked up at Mom, she was backing away as if I were now made of acid. Norovsambuu showed her impatience on her brow.

My limbs hesitant, I bent into a basic position.

"Okay," Norovsambuu said.

I lifted up into a chin-stand, which meant placing my ankles beside my shoulders—the exact position I had seen my idol take the first time I saw her on television. Norovsambuu said nothing. I tried to focus on her expression, search for some sign that she was impressed or unimpressed, but she held her skeptical gaze throughout, unflinching.

"Okay," she repeated. She stood with a start. "She can train with me."

My heart skipped several beats. At first, I wasn't sure whether I had heard her correctly. I stood.

Norovsambuu turned her attention to Mother. "If you bring her in tomorrow, she can begin."

Mom, quivering, stepped forward with both arms outstretched. Against some resistance, she took Norovsambuu's hands in hers and thanked her profusely. She kept thanking her as we backed out of the room, as if failure to appease her might cause her to change her mind. Where this might have annoyed or amused most people, Norovsambuu's expression did not change. She merely glared at us until we were out of sight.

The moment we backed into the hallway and the door closed between us, I turned to my mother and hugged her, squealing. I was so happy, I felt as if I might fly from the room, bursting through the ceiling, tile and two-by-fours and shingle toppling in every direction, born about by my wake.

On the way home, I noticed that Mom was crying behind the dark glasses she often wore.

"What's wrong?" I asked her.

"That's not the first time you and I have met Norovsambuu."

I cocked my head to one side, my body rocking in unison with my mother's, our weight shifted here and there by the inertia of the pockmarked roads.

"When you were five years old," Mom said, wiping a tear, "I took you to Norovsambuu's home to let her judge your potential as a contortionist. Do you remember that?"

I shook my head, furrowing my brow.

"Norovsambuu's parents lived in Zavkhan. They were neighbors to my parents. So that's how I knew her. Our parents grew up together."

I gazed out the window. The landscape passed in flat, dusty lines.

"So I went to her house one day and asked her mother, 'Please, please, can Norovsambuu teach my daughter?'"

"Her mother told me she would ask her and let me know."

After that, Mom smiled, her one good eye still brimming with tears.

"What did Norovsambuu say?"

Mom's smile faded. "She said you were too young to start training, but that I should bring you back when you turned eight."

I felt altogether disappointed. Here I was more than nine years old. Nearly ten, really. Mom seemed to sense what I was thinking.

"When you turned eight, Dad got sick, remember?" she said by way of defense.

I nodded vaguely.

"He needed constant bed rest. How was I supposed to take my daughter to practice when my husband required my attention at all hours of the day?"

I shrugged, still not really satisfied.

"Your sisters were in school and your brother in the army," Mom insisted. "Your other brother was way off in the countryside, and Noyo too. I was the only one who could take you to training. And when you were eight, I was busy."

We passed a half mile in silence—or as much silence as the whirring, rickety bus would allow. I kept pondering what I had already determined to be my unfortunate fate. To be robbed of two years of training by way of simple circumstance. I wondered then whether I would be older than Norovsambuu's other pupils by several years.

"That's why Noyo was so adamant," Mom said, a look of pride returning to her weathered but still lovely face. "Noyo said you had the talent and that we had to do something with you or risk having you end up with nothing."

My heart fluttered as I thought of my oldest sister. "So that's why I've been going to practice? Because Noyo insisted?"

Mother nodded, her lips taut and solemn.

Noyo. My big sister. She had set everything in motion. And thanks to her and Mother's tireless efforts to guide me to and from practice, I would catch my first real break in my career as a contortionist.

CHAPTER 4

From the time I was a little girl, if I wanted something, I would do whatever it took to get it. When I began training with Norovsambuu, my determination was pushed to its limits. My new coach proved herself to be incredibly disciplined. Even in an environment full of tough and demanding coaches, Norovsambuu was by far the toughest and most demanding. When I would fall, she would holler and make me try again. She would stalk back and forth as I trained, smacking her hand over her wrist in a show of frustration.

Despite her harsh tones and unflinching demeanor, I came to respect Norovsambuu in the way a little girl respects her mother: there was dislike there, yes, but it was overshadowed completely by an unbridled respect. I would usually bristle when yelled at, but I would never complain or refuse to do what was asked of me. For this reason, I learned a great deal of discipline and toughness in this stage of my life. And my abilities as a contortionist evolved quickly and accordingly.

Not until I was much older did I discover that Norovsambuu wasn't simply working me like a horse for my own benefit. The coaches at my school were apparently in direct competition with one another, and as a result, they all pushed their students to be the best. If they advanced the career of a young girl, their own careers would advance as well.

After training, I would come home with Mother, who would help me work on my new poses during what little free time I had. Sometimes she would get frustrated with me, saying things like, "If you can't learn, you shouldn't do it!" and "Just go to bed!" Of course, this would throw me into fits of anger that would prevent any measure of sleep.

Such was my determination that I would often forgo sleep to get better, anyway. There were times when I would wake up in the middle of the night to practice my latest pose. This happened most often whenever I came up against a particular pose that was beyond my current skill level. Mom would wake up and come to me.

"What's happening to you?" she would hiss. "Are you crazy? It's the middle of the night. Go to sleep!"

Despite what I had thought when we first rode home on the bus from my audition with the queen of all contortionism, Norovsambuu did not have many students. In fact, I was only one of two. My hero's first student was a young girl named Uugii.

Uugii was older than me by two years, and she had several inches in height to show for it. We both stood shorter than Norovsambuu— our most likely target in height, once we reached womanhood – but not by much. Uugii's had an unusual appearance, given that she was light skinned enough to be described as almost pale. She stood out with her dark brown hair and hazel eyes, so much so that many thought she looked like a Russian. Almost immediately upon meeting Uugii, I realized that my training partner was far more outgoing than me. In time, I would learn that she was able to talk her way out of any trouble she might get herself into.

Considering this enviable skill, Uugii seemed to draw less of Norovsambuu's angst, most likely because she was certainly not shy. Unlike me, she had no problem approaching our coach and talking woman to woman about problems she might be having. I was perhaps too quiet, which of course made it easier to blame me when things went wrong. I would simply absorb the blame and try to bury my anguish. Given that our coach was never happy, even when we performed well, there was an awful lot of blame to go around.

"Terrible," she would say whenever one of us would stumble. "You two are the worst contortionists in the building."

Only in the early going was this true. We might have started out poorly, but we ascended the ranks quicker than anyone could have expected. This was because we had the toughest coach, but also the greatest teacher.

More important than all that, Norovsambuu stood up for us—and in some of her more private moments, she even showed just how much she cared. Our coach had just left in a tizzy, her slender arms waving in the air as if she had never seen anything more infuriating in her life. We had been practicing in front of the other performers, and Norovsambuu had wanted, as always, perfection.

I was holding Uugii aloft, both my hands pressed to her steely stomach. Uugii had bent herself backward, grabbing both ankles with both hands above her head. Whether it was my lack of strength and focus or a subtle wobble from Uugii, I can't say, but I do know that my partner came toppling to the floor—which is what sent Norovsambuu mincing from the room.

It had been an impressive practice to that point. For as often as our coach yelled at me, I had been flawless. In just a few short months, I had made incredible strides. Many of the other students had watched us with something akin to awe.

When the slip happened and Norovsambuu stormed off, Uugii and I were left alone to finish our routine in front of the others. We quickly rocked back into position, and Uugii performed the last of her contortions in my steady grip. When we finished up, the other performers and coaches merely stood and dusted themselves off, heading for their dressing rooms to shower.

Uugii did the same. She walked a few steps ahead of me, turning to look over her slight shoulder to see if I would be joining. I shook my head and waved her off.

From the training room, I ran light on my toes, making the abrupt turn into the hall that would lead to our dressing room. I slid down the wall, straining to listen to the familiar voice of my coach. But when I reached Norovsambuu's door and pressed my ear to the thin wood, it would be Tuya's voice that I would hear first.

"Otgo was supposed to be mine," she said.

My heart leapt.

Norovsambuu laughed.

"I was going to take her from the MYTZ Ordon," Tuya insisted. "I wanted to make her *my* student."

My breathing quickened, drowning out Norovsambuu's voice as she replied. I tried to slow it despite my excitement as I pressed my ear closer to the door.

"… going to come to me with this now?" Norovsambuu said.

"Please," Tuya said, sounding almost as if she was begging, "can you give this girl to me?"

Norovsambuu laughed. "No. I can't do that."

"But I had every intention of—"

"Tuya," Norovsambuu interrupted, "the girl comes to me at my mother's request."

"But—"

"Even if I wanted to give her to you, I couldn't. I train her as a favor."

I heard footsteps on the floor, shuffling in my direction. I left the door, jogging toward the bend in the hall in the hopes of avoiding being discovered as Tuya exited the office.

Back in the hallway, I caught my breath, my heart racing and my smile so wide I could scarcely see. For all her posturing and insulting, Norovsambuu *did* want me. And more than that, other coaches wanted me too. As frustrating as my training had been to that point, I felt for the first time that I might actually have a future in this business.

———

In my country, any artist who hopes to become a professional must first perform a small, solo show in the countryside. My tryout show would fall on February 2nd of 1981. I remember little about the show, save for the fact that I was good enough to be named an official supporting artist for my contortionist troupe. My excitement could hardly be contained.

More than my excitement over being named to the company was my excitement over receiving my first paycheck.

In Mongolia at the time, there were different pay grades for performance artists based on their level of experience and skill. Everyone began as I did: as a supporting artist, or *Dagaldan Jujegchen*. These people would receive the relatively small amount of 150 Togrog per month. It wasn't until you were named a true professional contortionist that you would make a reasonable living.

Of course, when I was almost eleven years old, I didn't care about the inequity in pay-grade. I only cared that I was going to be receiving real money to do the thing that I loved. So it was with ludicrous excitement that I bounced into the long line of performers on payday.

I stared down the line. Everyone was still dressed in their practice tights, and to my eye, it seemed like there were more people present than I could ever remember seeing. Mom wasn't there on that day, as Dad had taken another turn for the worse in his illness. After two years of riding the bus with her, she finally trusted me to do it alone, anyway.

So I bounced and bubbled alone. I asked every question about payday that I could think of to anyone who would listen. Anyone who wished to listen would tell me to quit flapping my lips and just wait silently like everyone else.

With every sudden jolt of the line, my heart would skip. I would crane my neck around the much taller performers in front of me, trying to eyeball the table toward which everyone headed. By the time I got within four or five positions from the front, I finally spotted what was going on. At a desk sat a woman in bureaucratic spectacles. She had a stack of paperwork to her left and a large organizer to her right. Just as I looked, she reached into the organizer, producing a stack of bills, which she handed to the young performer at the head of the line. The performer moved in orderly fashion toward the door.

The line shifted forward. My heart skipped.

The next several minutes would be the longest in my life, but finally, I reached the head of the line. The bureaucrat looked me over as I bounced in place, rubbing my hands together. She rolled her eyes and checked her paperwork. Her long, bony finger traced downward over the topmost paper in the stack.

"Otgo," she spat.

I lit up.

The bureaucrat issued an epic sigh. Then she turned to the organizer and fingered a short stack of cash into her left hand. "One hundred fifty T," she said, sorting the money. "You have to sign." She pointed in a huff to the paper in the center of the table.

I signed the paper, snapped up the cash, and bolted for the door.

I ran from the building and made my way into the waning light of the evening. I plodded along a road of shattered concrete, passing row after row of square-shouldered buildings. When I came to my bus stop, I kept running.

I clutched my money in my fist, and I ran. Several miles separated me from home, but I knew I could never wait for a bus in the state I was in. I couldn't wait. Never in my life had I wanted something more than I wanted to hand that sweaty wad of money to my mother. So I ran. I ran as hard and for as long as I could along that unfinished, bumpy road. I stopped to catch my breath when I needed to, but apart from those few moments, I ran.

I had made this trip hundreds of times in two years, most of the time by bus. My joints ached and my muscles burned by the time my ger came into view.

"Mom!" I yelled, short of breath.

Mom came out from inside our ger, shielding her eye from the low-lying sun.

"Mom! Mom!"

Mother leapt to the gate, pushing through and waiting for me in the road. "Otgo! What happened?"

I reached her, my hands falling to my knees as I panted for breath.

"Did something happen to you?"

Still doubled over, I lifted my hand, still closed tightly around the money. I looked up at my mother, who stared at the bills with something like a horrified eye.

"Where did you get that money?" she barked. "You know how I feel about stealing."

"No!" I hollered with an exhausted smile. "I got paid today."

Mom smiled down at me, her green eye lolling. "My baby," she whispered. "She worked so hard, and now she will be able to put food on the table for her family."

She took me into her arms. I cried with joy.

"Our blessed baby," Mom said to the heavens.

I hugged her tightly. "Mom," I said into her chest, "please go to the grocery store."

"I will," Mom breathed. "Right away."

I pulled away and beamed up at her. "Buy some meat today. Some milk. Some noodles. We should have a proper dinner."

I could see from her expression that she resisted at first, but when she looked at the money again, she brightened up. "Okay, honey." She then turned and hobbled up the road, looking back at me now and then to smile.

"Otgo!" came a voice from inside the house. It was my father.

I ran to him, finding him lying in bed on his side.

"Khumban Tsagaan oxen," he said, shaking his head with pride as he used my nickname. He kissed me on my forehead, and when he pulled away, I saw him smile for the first time since he had come down from the mountain.

My sisters were speechless when I told them.

Mom came back from the store. She had bought cookies and candies, which she handed over to us in turn. We all cheered. I checked her bags for the other things I had asked for, but she shook her head dolefully.

"They were sold out of meat and milk," she said. "These cookies were all they had."

I frowned, disappointed, but in the end, I didn't much care. We had something to eat, and it was plentiful. We ate everything that Mom had brought, our stomachs bulging, our heads swimming with sugar. It would have been nice to have a decent meal on my first payday, but in Socialist Mongolia, the grocery never had much to choose from. They only sold certain items on certain days. Meat and milk were only sold in the morning, so the idea that there would be any for Mother to buy in the late evening was ridiculous to begin with.

I rubbed my belly, hoping Mom would have enough money to return the next day. I pictured her waiting in the vast lines that would form outside the store every morning, a great stack of bills in her hand for the first time in her life. I pictured her wading through the chaos that always ensued when the grocery store first opened its doors each morning, a smile on her face and pride for her little girl lining her heart.

—◦◦◦—

With cash coming in monthly now—and Mom putting some money aside with each new payment—life got slowly better for my family. My siblings and I were obviously very happy to have square meals every day and night, but the biggest turning point for us was when Mom managed to save up enough money to buy a refrigerator.

I remember the day we wheeled it home, our brand new, Russian-made Zil 130.

"Oh, yes," Dad said when he first laid eyes on the boxy beauty. "This is top-of-the-line. Best refrigerator there is."

"Now our food won't go bad so easily in the spring and summer," Mom said.

"And you won't have to dig the hole in the winter!" I said, referring to the makeshift cellar my sisters would have to construct in the yard before each year's first frost.

Everyone nodded at that.

Together, Mom, Naraa, Enkhee, and I pushed through the yard the cart bearing our new refrigerator, our sickly father standing watch with his hands on his hips.

—◦◦◦—

Each season would bring a new tour for the performers at the Mongolian State Circus. In the winter, with buses unreliable, roads terrible, and temperatures dropping well below freezing, we would travel by plane. We would take first a white plane from Ulaanbaatar's airport, then a rickety green biplane from whatever tiny connecting airport we were routed through.

For the spring, summer, and fall tours, we would travel in a sometimes cramped bus. Regardless of where we were going, we would always pack every performer and all the equipment needed for the performance onto one bus. Sometimes, there were only seven or eight people. Other times, it was more like fifteen to seventeen.

Some tours would feature a little train travel, which was always my favorite. Trains are so much more spacious and luxurious than buses or airplanes.

The trips would always depart from the State Circus in Ulaanbaatar and would typically last either a month or forty-five days. Where and when we stopped was entirely up to the government, who had assigned directors to handle that sort of thing.

My first tour happened to be a winter tour, so we would travel by plane between stops along the countryside. I always preferred the countryside tours to the city or international tours, because the daily life was much simpler. We would travel from town to town, arriving in the late afternoon, setting up and then performing two or three shows in the evening. When we finished, we would have dinner in whatever small hotel the latest town could offer. Most of them were simple hotels, but they always had the nicest food. Growing up as poor as I was, I always relished the opportunity to eat fresh meat, dumplings, beef stew—whatever they had to offer for the touring circus performers.

While on tour, we were kept almost constantly busy with all the setting up and performing. But while on the road, there was plenty of idle time. Most of the older performers would pass the time by playing cards or other games near the back of the bus. Mongolians love to sing as well, so the troupe would often break out in spontaneous measures of song. Since I was young and still in school, I passed most of my drive time by reading or doing my homework. The bus was always enjoyable, happy—the other performers always nice.

At the end of my first forty-five days touring the countryside, our group returned to Ulaanbaatar, where we were tasked to assemble the New Year's performance for the State Circus. For my first year, the show would be directed at children. Our director would base the show on a famous story about a magical clock. To my great surprise, I would be chosen for the honor of passing through the clock during the peak moment of the show. This would be the biggest challenge of my life, and it would come at a remarkably young age. It would be my first opportunity to become a professional artist: the real deal.

At that time, given that Mongolia was a Socialist country, everything was subject to government approval. This included the stylistic decisions for circus shows, from the sets right down to the performers. *The Magical Clock* was a relatively new story, so our director had to endure many different governmental checks and balances. One of the final hurdles required that we all perform for the Ministry of Culture. After the show, the ministry would have a meeting and decide whether they would approve the show. Many times, if they didn't like something, they would tell the producers to make a change.

Our show before the ministry would be held at the State Circus. Our audience would be small but comprised almost solely of influential people. There was a special level of nerves passing from performer to performer when we learned that Tsedenbal Filatova herself—the Russian wife of our country's political leader—would be attending the show. She was quite the figurehead for our government, so there wasn't a single performer who didn't want to give the performance of her life in front of Filatova.

Fifteen minutes before the show would begin, I was getting ready behind the curtains. I had just warmed myself up into one of the simpler postures I would perform on the night when Inspector Nyamaa, a high-profile member of the ministry, came up to me and tapped me on the hipbone.

I stood from my bend and welcomed him with downcast eyes.

"You won't be performing this show," he said.

My heart dropped.

"Tuya and Erka will perform their duo act only."

I wanted to argue, but knew that I could not. My culture would not permit such things.

To his credit, Nyamaa seemed to notice the protest in my posture, for he explained himself. "Mrs. Filatova is in attendance." He placed his hand on my shoulder. "You are too new and too young to perform for such an audience."

I felt numb as I stood before the inspector.

"What are you doing?" he said after a time. "Don't just stand there. Go! Go!"

I dropped my head and walked back to my dressing room, put my clothes on, and went home.

The next day, Norovsambuu learned what had happened. I couldn't recall ever seeing her so upset.

"Conspiracy!" she howled to me.

I was too young to understand what she meant.

"I'll get to the bottom of this," she said, storming from her dressing room.

CHAPTER 5

When I first began training at the State Circus, Norovsambuu was still a regular performer in many of the country's shows. As a result, she would travel a great deal. Every time she went away, she would instruct me to train with other coaches. This made learning rather difficult, as every coach's training skills were different. But really, I had no other choice.

Of course, because of the tremendous competition between each coach, whenever Norovsambuu would return, there would be a great deal of bickering about what I had and hadn't learned. My coach would often spend a good portion of her first few sessions with me deconstructing everything another coach had spent a week or more teaching me.

On one occasion when Norovsambuu was away, I was set to perform for the minister of foreign affairs. While I was getting ready in my dressing room, an older contortionist named Erka strolled in and told me that I was to listen to her for the evening.

"Otgo," she said, "I know you're supposed to do this show, but I really wanted this show. You should let me do it."

I scoffed. "If I don't do this show, my coach will be mad at me." I pulled my tights over my left leg and then struggled into my right.

Erka's face melted to an improbable look of empathy. "You don't have to worry about a thing. I'll talk to her."

"I'm sorry," I said. "I can't do that."

The moment the words left my lips, Erka began to cry. The tears came softly, at first, but before I had even had the chance to pull my tights up, she tumbled to her knees, sobbing. She grasped my wrists, gripping hard.

"You have to help me," she said in fits.

I tried to pull my arms away, but to no avail. Erka clasped my hand in hers.

"I'm falling in love," she said.

I felt more uncomfortable than I had ever felt, but I couldn't pull away.

"He works for the Ministry of Foreign Affairs," Erka explained. "He doesn't even know I exist."

"Why don't you go talk to him?" I asked girlishly.

"No!" Erka hollered, staring up at me. Then, just as quickly as her anger had come, it faded back to desperation. "If you let me do this show, I will perform well for my love. Maybe then I'll have a chance to meet him."

I scoffed again. Even to my childish mind, the whole thing sounded ludicrous.

"I really, really love him, Otgo," Erka sobbed. "Soon, you will fall in love with someone too. Then you'll understand how I feel."

I sighed, my shoulders slumping. I wrenched my arms free and lifted her chin. "Go," I said.

Her face began to light.

"Go," I repeated. "Go ahead and do it."

"Are you sure, Otgo?" she asked, standing slowly.

"Yes, yes."

She bolted from the room, arms flailing.

—◦◦◦—

With the Magical Clock New Year show behind me—and having been a roaring success in my performance—I was invited to travel abroad to Hungary for an International Circus Show.

The day I informed my parents, they were overwhelmed with excitement. Mom's eye brimmed with tears and Dad couldn't stop shaking his head. The slightest smile held on the corner of his lips, and in it, I saw pride. Mother kissed my cheek. Father asked how long I would be gone.

"Two months," I said with glee.

The mood became decidedly more somber. I pulled away from Mother.

"Two *months?*" Dad said.

I nodded.

"What will we do without you here?"

I didn't know what to say.

"Who is going to look out for you while you're on the road?" Mom asked, clearly disheartened.

"It's okay, Mom," I said, smiling. "They'll assign me a chaperone, I'm sure."

The three of us stood in silence for a time. With my eyes, I tried urging my parents to ignore the obvious pitfalls and see that this was a giant step forward in my career.

"Okay," Mom said, nodding at Father. "You can go as long as you have a chaperone."

I thanked my parents to no end, and that night, we all went to bed happy.

The next morning, with my rusty old trunk packed and ready, I would learn that I would indeed have a chaperone—a fifty-year-old crone named Tseky. Her skin was the color of dates, her eyes narrow and black as pitch.

It was early springtime, perhaps April of 1982. Ms. Tseky and I flew from Ulaanbaatar to Erkutska to Moscow. On the plane, we were served hot food. I was nervous when the stewardess set the tray on the table before me because this was the first time I had ever flown overseas and certainly the first time I had ever eaten food aboard a plane. The meal, of course, was a chicken leg, so I had a grand time carving it with knife and fork in ladylike fashion.

I glanced across the aisle at Tseky, who was already chomping down on a healthy cut of meat, her fork and knife held blade-up. I longed to eat with such abandon, but my upbringing wouldn't allow it. I slid my fork into my chicken leg, and I brought the knife to the meat.

The plane lurched. I stiffened and dropped an oyster of chicken into my lap. My lips began to quiver with embarrassment. Tseky shook her head.

When we landed in Moscow's Sheremetyevo Airport, we had a couple of hours to wait for our next flight into Budapest. Tseky passed the time by reading a magazine. With permission from my chaperone, I decided to wander the airport.

I strolled around the terminal with wide eyes. My career had taken me to many different places, but I had never seen anything like Sheremetyevo Airport before. It was like a giant, sterile, softly lit shopping mall. The duty-free stores were crammed with people, all of them carrying heavy bags. I wanted desperately to enter, but being as young as I was, I thought I had to have money even to set foot inside. So, penniless, I stood outside the glass façade, staring through the store window at women and children buying candy, chocolate, and gum—all with this strange green money.

I could smell the perfumes, even from the hall. They brought my senses to dance in ways I had never experienced. The sound of laughter and of the cash register sparked my heart to skip. The children passing by with chocolate caused my mouth to water.

Will I ever be this lucky? I asked myself. *Will I ever live like these rich foreigners?*

That day, I formed for myself a new dedication. If it was the last thing I did, I would use my talents as a contortionist to move up in the world. *Someday,* I thought, *I will use that green money to buy all the candy and chocolate I can stand.*

I returned from Hungary having performed a successful series of shows. I found the city lovely and old, its people lively and blunt. But as much as I enjoyed seeing new sights, I was glad to return home.

Unfortunately, I would return home to poor news. Father had grown sicker during my absence, and every day, the problem worsened. We had all lived with Dad's illness for a long time, of course, but a new kind of pall hung over the family on that first night back home. I had just given everyone the presents I had brought back from Hungary—purchased with the money I had earned performing my shows—when Mom placed her hands on the table and darkened her mood.

"Your father is not doing well," she said.

My sisters and I sat in silence, wondering what else was new.

"I hate to say this," Mom continued, turning away, "but I think we have to prepare for …"

She couldn't continue. Naraa cried. Enkhee asked why. Mom didn't answer. I felt a lump form in the back of my throat.

I didn't go to work for a full week after learning the news. Such was my devastation at the thought of losing the man who had always been the bedrock of our family. But the time came when I wouldn't be able to avoid training any longer. So at my mother's urging, I returned to the circus building.

That night was the most difficult night of training I had ever had. The moment it finished and Norovsambuu excused me, I rushed from the building and ran home. This was the first time I had forgone the bus since the day I received my first paycheck, but unlike the first run home, my muscles didn't ache this time. I was simply too deep in thought and emotional pain to notice anything else.

When I rounded the corner into my neighborhood, our ger came into view. Standing just outside, halfway between the fence and the front door, was Enkhee. Her slender lips sagged at the corners.

"I have to tell you something," she said as I stood with hands on knees, catching my breath.

I nodded.

"Dad just passed away."

I fell to my knees and clutched at my sister's dress. She held my hands for a moment. She sat down next to me in the snow. She ran her hand over my sweaty hair. She rocked me slowly. I cried.

The date was November 3, 1982. That was the day my world turned upside down.

"I don't believe you!" I yelled at my sister, sobbing.

"Please," Enkhee said softly. "I know it hurts. It hurts so badly. But we knew he was very sick for a long time. We knew he wouldn't be with us long."

"But that doesn't make it easy!"

Enkhee rocked me for a moment, caressing my head. "No, it doesn't," she said after a time.

From the moment I stepped foot in the house until sunset on the third day after Father's death, Mother was a busy mess. She had to contact everyone in the family and all our friends and ask them to assemble in our neighborhood. In Mongolian tradition, usually when a person dies, he or she must be buried within three days after death. But burials are only allowed on certain days during the week: Monday, Wednesday, and Friday. Regardless of the day chosen, the attire would be strictly black and red.

On a Wednesday, we buried my father at the nearest cemetery. This was my first burial. I didn't know how to deal with situations like these. I felt numb and pained at the same time. And for the longest time, I blamed myself for Father's death. If only I had been there when he passed away.

At the time, I assumed that the most difficult thing about losing a parent is saying goodbye at the burial. And I was right. But what I didn't know was that the second most difficult thing—and it was a close second—was dealing with an empty house after everyone departed.

In my country, in those days, there was no such thing as a grief counselor or psychiatrist. So my sisters and I clung especially hard to the family and friends who had come to visit and pay their respects to Father. When they departed, we were left with only each other. Enkhee had by now moved on to her own ger, and Naraa was in high school and never home. So that left just me and Mom. The loneliness was the most difficult thing I had ever experienced.

Mom talked about Dad as often as she could. The conversations were often light, but always one-sided. I was shy to begin with, and also a teenager, so I had a tendency to keep everything bottled up inside. In many ways, those days would change me forever. When I lost my father, I felt like I'd lost a part of my own spirit. It left a hole that I would spend many long years trying to fill.

CHAPTER 6

Because we lived in a ger, bath time in the tub obviously made for little privacy, which was a problem for me in those days, being a teenage girl. Sometimes, I would invite myself over to my friend's house to use the shower her family had in their apartment.

Our ger did not have access to a water line. So when we needed water for drinking, cooking, or taking a bath, we would have to fetch our water from the neighborhood's lone *khudag* (which was a well of spring water). We would lift one of two forty-liter buckets from the well, struggle to walk it down the street, and bring it inside to dump in the tub. When my sisters were home, we used to get the water together, but after they went on to college, I had to do everything myself. I didn't want to let Mother do it, given her advanced age.

Every two weeks, the garbage car would visit our neighborhood. They would stop in the middle of the street, and I would have to drag our two big buckets of trash out to them. Since I was so small, I could only drag one bucket at a time, so I would have to rush to get the second one or the men would leave. Much of the trash I would carry out twice monthly would be ash from the coal we would burn in our stove. The ashes would kick up on the wind and pepper me in white. Some days, when the breezes were strong, Mother would chuckle at me when I returned to the ger, saying I looked like a ghost.

Once monthly, every neighborhood used to have a meeting to determine courses of action on given problems and also to dole out the latest instructions from the government. It used to be Mother's job to go to these meetings, but one day when I was thirteen, she told me to go in her stead.

"Why don't you go today?" she said, pushing me gently toward the door.

"Okay," I said, shrugging. "But I have no idea what to do."

"Don't worry," Mom said. "You'll be fine. Just go."

When I arrived at the center, I found that the square, concrete building was flanked by a line of people. I gasped. I had no idea that we had so many people in our neighborhood, let alone so many people who would want to attend one of these meetings. I stepped into line, keeping silent, my eyes trained on the trench coat before me.

When I reached the door into the building, I didn't know what to do, so I simply followed the man who had been standing in front of me in line. He took a seat in the second row, and I sat beside him. As everyone else filed in, I studied the room. It was drab and square. A single wooden podium stood atop a rickety, low-lying stage.

I turned around to look at faces. Most everyone was blowing into their hands from the cold. Some smiled at one another, greeting old friends. Others stared silently ahead, anxious for the meeting to begin. When I sat back and looked ahead, the first thing my eyes settled upon was an older man with a bald, round head, just like my father's. My heart leapt. Wanting to make sure that I wasn't seeing a ghost, I stared at the man. The woman sitting beside him said something to him, and he turned to reply. My heart leapt again. He had the same brow, the same nose, and the same lips as my father.

A thin middle-aged man stepped to the podium and began to speak, but I could scarcely hear a word he was saying, my concentration on my father's doppelganger was so intense. I learned nothing at the meeting—and later, when my mother would ask me what it was about, I wouldn't have a reply. The only thing on my mind was the old man.

When the meeting finally came to an end, I tapped the old man on the shoulder. He turned, and with a kindly smile, he said hello.

"Hello," I said.

"How do you do?" he said, his smile broadening.

I felt short of breath. Even his voice was similar to my father's. "You look so much like my dad," I said.

"That's a good thing, I hope."

"I lost him not long ago."

"Oh," the old man said, his voice soft now and delicate.

We stared at one another for a time. The old man appeared uncomfortable at first, but then he brightened up.

"Where do you live?" he asked.

I gave him my street number.

"I know where that is," he said. "What are your parents' names?"

"My father's name was Adiya," I said. "My mother's name is Buted."

The old man nodded, showing no sign of whether he had heard the names before. His eyes became vacant, as if he had lost the thread of the conversation, but then, his lips tensed and he nodded toward the door. "Are you here by yourself?"

"Yes," I said. "I came alone."

The old man frowned. "Well, my name is Sharav, and I could never live with myself if I let such a young girl walk home alone, as dark and cold as it is."

I nodded.

"You should never go out by yourself, young lady."

I nodded, more vigorously this time.

"Let me take you home."

The old man stood and offered his arm, which I took in my tiny hands. Together, we made our way toward the crowd being ushered through the door. We spoke without stopping as Sharav walked me home. I recited stories of my father, and he told me that he seemed like a caring and honorable man.

"Quite a man to look like," he quipped.

As melancholy as I was to be walking with my dead father's twin, I laughed.

Before I knew it, we were standing on the corner of my street. My ger was in sight, the lights burning low.

"Would you like to come in?" I asked.

"Oh no," the old man said. "I wouldn't want to impose."

"No, I insist. My mother will want to meet you."

Sharav furrowed his brow in obvious concern. "Because I look like your—"

"Because you walked me home," I interrupted with a smile.

Sharav nodded knowingly and followed me into the yard. At our front door, I knocked. This seemed to confuse my companion, but I didn't bother explaining that knocking wasn't usual protocol—that I merely wanted to ensure that my mother was decent before I came barging in with a stranger.

After a few short moments, Mother answered the door, bearing a deeply confounded look. Her eye bobbed in her head as she glared at me.

"Why would you knock?" she asked.

I indicated my new friend.

Mom's stern gaze drifted to the stranger. When she took him in, she appeared to lose her balance for a moment. "Hello," she said.

"My name is Sharav," the old man said. "You should never let your daughter go by herself at night."

Mom gasped through a little laugh. She seemed incapable of tearing her eyes from the man who looked so much like her departed husband. "I was going to walk over and accompany her home, but I didn't expect the meeting to end so early."

The two of them stared at each other for some time before Mom finally came down from the shock and invited Sharav inside.

This is how I met the man who helped me get through the grieving over my father and the healing that would need to occur. Of course, no matter how often he visited, Sharav's main concern was that we didn't think of him as Father's replacement. As a result, I began to call him Grandpa, a name that suited him just fine.

In the weeks that followed, Grandpa proved to be an amazingly capable man, one who was as wise and as down to earth as anyone I had ever met. He had three grown sons.

"No daughters?" I asked him one day at the dinner table.

"I had a daughter, yes," he said. "She died when she was twenty years old."

"And your wife?" Mom asked.

"She died shortly after my daughter," Grandpa said, his eyes glistening sadly.

A tear rolled down my cheek.

"So it's just me and my boys now," he said.

As the weeks became months, Grandpa would get a chance to meet everyone else in the family. And with every new brother or sister he met, he became closer to the family. In almost no time at all, he became more like the grandfather that his nickname suggested and less like the familiar-looking stranger who had walked me home from the neighborhood meeting.

Each year, the State Circus would perform a traveling show called *Bargiad*. This was one of the shows that would traverse the countryside by bus. At thirteen years old, this was my third or fourth trip across the countryside, but I remained the youngest of the group and certainly the only child.

Our first stop would be in Nalaikh, a small town near Ulaanbaatar. There, we performed in the tiny Klub Theater, where we, both males and females, shared small dressing rooms. For the older women, changing costumes in front of the men was not a problem. They had seen and been seen by nude men before, after all. But for me, I had a difficult time. Not only was I inexperienced with men, but it was a time in my life when my body was undergoing a number of embarrassing changes.

Whenever we all entered the dressing rooms to change, I would hide behind a curtain, pulling on my wardrobe out of sight. On one such occasion, I had only just removed my trousers, and stood now fully nude, when someone rushed forward and pulled the curtain back.

I screamed, snatching up my shirt and trying to cover my body. I pulled my bent leg in front of the other, clutching at my chest with one hand and my thighs with the other, willing the shirt to lengthen. When I looked up with dewy eyes, I saw Altai, an older female performer. She stared down at me with a dark and judgmental gaze.

"Why are you hiding behind the curtain?" she asked.

At that moment, the shirt I was holding drooped, exposing my breasts. Altai cackled.

"Oh, I see!" she said loudly, wheeling around to project her findings to the rest of the room. "Spring is arriving! Flowers are blooming!" She turned around to look at me again, a terrible smile etched across her face. "And you, my little sister … your breasts are growing!" She fell back into wild laughter.

The other men and women in the room joined in.

Altai sashayed away from me, singing a familiar song about a baby camel, changing the words to suit my girlish nudity. The laughter grew raucous.

One of the men swooped in and took a good long look at my breasts. "Oh yeah!" he said flatly. "Flowers are blooming!"

"Such chalky white skin," said another man, hopping in to pretend to pinch me.

I screeched and toppled into the wall behind me. My blush was substantial. I hated my body in that moment. Hated my broadening hips, my growing breasts. Hated the hair my mother had given me, so black and so lovely. Hated the lips I had inherited from my mother, the skin and eyes I had gained from my father. But more than everything I hated about myself, I hated the leers from the men in the room. Chief among them was a man in his early fifties, one of the most respected performers in the troupe. He stood only a shade taller than most of the women, but

I could make out his hungry gaze even from his darkened corner on the opposite side of the room.

This was a slender man of dark skin. This was a man of thinning gray hair that jutted from either side of a round head. This was a man with a face decorated with red paint on the tip of his nose and both cheeks. This was Sanaa the Clown.

CHAPTER 7

F̲ollowing the first truly embarrassing moment of my young life, every time I would change into my costume, I would find Sanaa standing nearby. He would never make himself apparent intentionally, but I could always detect his frame silhouetted in the rosy red curtain that hung between us. I would hear him grunt as he applied his face-paint, see his shadow rocking whenever I noticed a flash of the curtain out of the corner of my eye.

Sanaa was the oldest man in the show, and so was well respected. Apart from missing several of his front teeth, he boasted a harmless look. His eyes were dark, but always kind to the other performers. Whenever they leveled on me, they looked hungry.

One day, I was running behind on my wardrobe. I heard much of the room begin to clear out, even as I had just begun to change. There, against the curtain, I could see Sanaa's outline. I bent to gather my costume. I heard the curtain whirl back. Horrified, I bent to shield my body. I craned my neck to look the clown in the eye. He licked his fat lips.

"My sweet little sister," he said, salivating as he reached out one grubby hand, "let your brother touch your pretty breast."

Squealing, I turned away from his grip. "What are you talking about?" I hollered.

"Please!" he said, his voice oily and strained. "Please let me touch you."

I screamed, clenching my eyes tight. The last I saw of the clown, his hand was extending toward me. I braced for the unwelcome paw. But it did not come. When I opened my eyes, he was gone. I stood alone, naked, in the dressing room, tears falling over my rouged cheeks.

Of course, there was no one I could talk to about the incident. I had a chaperone, yes, but I was young, and Sanaa was a respected performer. He had been traveling for many years with these people. No one would believe me.

Beyond his unassailable stature, I just didn't want to stir up any trouble for myself. I was the new girl, the young girl, the one still trying desperately to be accepted by her elders and heroes. So I kept it to myself. I hid my secret, and Sanaa's, praying that he would let it be.

I did my best to avoid him after that, but there is only so much avoiding one can do in close quarters. I kept to the crowds, noting that Sanaa only approached me when I was alone.

He would never say much. He would merely stare at me like a hungry wolf, grinding his teeth and grunting.

I would always pretend not to notice him, would always make for the nearest door or crowd. We passed the rest of the tour in this strange little dance, Sanaa always trying to steal moments with me as I tried to steal away from him. Finally, the tour came to an end—and with it, my relief washed over me in waves.

When I returned home, I considered telling my mother or sister or coach about what had happened, but something held me silent. Inside, I felt turmoil, and yet I couldn't bring myself to speak about why. It is a strange thing, fear. It grips you in the most unexpected and irrational ways. I was barely a teenager; I was a public performer; I was the sole breadwinner for my family; and I was frightened to death of the repercussions of confronting my issues with a clown. I simply kept my head down and hoped that Sanaa would forget about me and find something else to cling to now that we were home.

But my nightmare had yet to find its end. When Norovsambuu was around me, Sanaa would be elsewhere. Other times, he would come up to us and say things that would cause even the steeliest of women to swoon. He was always nice to me in the presence of other elders. Whenever he found me alone, he would try to grab at my breast or pinch my ass. He would moan in a way that made my skin crawl and my stomach lurch. He would say things so dirty and nasty that they made no sense to me at that age.

One morning, I was dragging my feet as I prepared to leave for school, my school bag slung over my shoulder, my head hung low.

"What's wrong, Otgo?" Mother asked me, her eyebrows taut and fine.

I shook my head, slogging for the door. Mom stepped in front of me.

"No, no," she said. "What's the matter?" She took my chin in her fingers, but I pulled my head away.

"Nothing!" I barked.

"It's not nothing!"

A vision of Sanaa the Clown came to my mind's eye, his dark eyes laughing, his vile breath wafting as a green mist through the gaps in his teeth. My heart wanted desperately to tell my mother what was going on in training. My eyes burned to cry. But instead, I stomped my feet and glared at the floor. "Just let me by."

"You're always so cheerful in the morning," Mother said as I pushed past.

As I scampered up the walk, I heard the door crack shut behind me. Then the hinges sang their ugly song. Mother had come outside to watch me leave. Without even looking, I knew the concern on her face. I could imagine her crossing her arms over her slight chest as she often did, shaking her head in worry.

———✺———

Winter came, bringing along with it the usual countryside tour for me and a handful of the performers from my troupe. The tour was set to last forty-five days. As was always the case, the leadership of the circus would hand-print the names of the performers selected for the tour and post them on a big board just outside the offices wing.

I pushed into the gathering crowd around the board, scanning for my name. I found it near the middle, nodding once and solemnly. Just as I turned to slide my way out, a thought occurred to me. I looked back and scanned the board again. There, my nightmare revealed itself. Sanaa's name had been chosen as well. Chills crept up my spine. I could practically feel his disgusting breath on the back of my neck already.

I ran to my coach to see who would be assigned as my guardian. It would be a woman I knew, an acrobat who also happened to be a wonderful person. I felt some measure of relief in knowing that she would be around, but in truth, I wasn't sure why the relief came. In my youthful mind at that time, Sanaa was little more than a nuisance—a creep who just wouldn't give me a moment of peace. It never occurred to me that a grown man would be capable of anything more than that when it came to a child. So my guardian, I believed, would be there only to prevent the clown from saying disturbing things. I considered approaching her about the problem right away, but with the crowd and the many idle ears, I didn't want to get into trouble.

A meeting was called shortly after the day's practice had ended. All the performers bound for the countryside tour were to meet in the director's room. I had no desire to attend, but knew that I must. The moment I passed into the director's room, I saw him. Sanaa the Clown. Sanaa the Nightmare. Without his face paint, he almost looked more clownish than when he performed his act. The single lightbulb that hung from the ceiling cast deep shadows across his wrinkled, angular face. He folded and unfolded his hands compulsively. He licked his lips. His gaze never left me as I found my seat.

The seat I chose was as far away from Sanaa as I could possibly manage. With Sanaa in the far corner, I found my chair right beside the door. All the other performers who entered behind me had to step over my legs and then shuffle down the wall to find a place to sit or stand. Once everyone had crammed inside, one of the circus administrators began speaking about the tour to come. He explained that, due to the winter weather, we would be traveling from small town to small town by an airplane called a *Nogoon Ongots*, which was a small green aircraft similar to a helicopter. I'm not entirely sure what else was said because I wasn't paying attention. I was too busy trying to remain small and quiet and out of Sanaa's sight.

The clown seemed to be doing his level best to make me uncomfortable. Every time I would shoot a glance his way, he would flash his hungry grin. He would thumb his nose. Hold his hand over his heart. Every gesture, every glance made me weak and sick. I wanted desperately not to look at him, but I couldn't control myself. It was like looking at a car accident—terrifying to behold, but too compelling to look away.

The moment the meeting was adjourned, I bolted through the door and to the women's dressing room. Alone or not, the clown could never encroach on me here.

The day the tour left, Mother stood with me at the stop for the bus that would bear me to the airport. My largest duffel rested at my ankles.

"You look troubled," Mom said.

I shook my head, my dark locks swaying.

"Are you worried you'll be homesick?"

I frowned, shaking my head again. I had been away for long stretches before, so it was a silly question. And in my troubled state of mind, I actually pitied my mother for asking it.

"You miss your father," she insisted.

I shrugged. I did miss my father, but the truth was that only one thing clouded my thoughts in those days. The rumble of the bus carried from around the corner on the wind. My mouth dropped open as I craned my neck to see its approach. I didn't want to leave my mother, but at that moment, as she asked her prodding questions, I didn't want to be around her, either.

"You haven't been the same since he passed."

I fell back on my heels. I bent down to pick up my duffel. I hugged my mother goodbye.

The bus screeched to a halt beside us. I hugged my mother again and then boarded the bus.

Though this was only a neighborhood bus, my eyes still darted back and forth over the seats, searching for my tormentor. I had no idea where Sanaa lived, but my paranoia had me believing that he could find me at any moment. Every dark corner, every occupied seat, held the potential for Sanaa.

On the plane, I sat as far away from the clown as I could manage. In the first city of the tour, I kept away from him. The same would go for the second city. And the third. For the first couple of weeks of the tour, Sanaa left me alone completely. In time, I found that my fear was replaced with tremendous relief. Maybe he had forgotten his little game with me. Maybe he wouldn't bother me anymore.

With my relief came complacency. I relaxed. I would wander around the halls of our hotels with or without my guardian. At night, after most of our shows, many of the performers would get together in one room or another and drink. I would attend these parties, trying my level best not to seem so young and naïve.

In the smaller towns, we would often have to share hotel rooms, many women in one room and many men in another. On these occasions, we would lump our belongings together in one corner.

On one such night, everyone was drinking in the boss's room. The boss was not someone who ever wanted to see a young girl like me drinking, so I wasn't sure what to do.

"Just go to bed and sleep," my guardian said. "You look tired, anyway."

I nodded and let her go on without me. I walked slowly down the dark hallway, feeling the chill from outside creep through the thin walls. I knew that a giant, dark, empty room awaited me, and I knew fear. As exhausted as I was from that evening's double-show, I would have trouble finding sleep.

I sought my cot along the near wall. With my head facing the door, I slipped under the tattered blanket. The cot creaked under my weight. I rolled onto my side, facing the wall, and closed my eyes. My heart raced. My mind bounced from one horrible thought to another. Outside, men and women were drinking. I was alone in a large, dark room.

The walls began to drip like dew from moss. The musty smell of earth reached my nostrils. A crow cawed overhead. Without realizing it, I had fallen into a dream. I lay now in a bed of damp leaves on a dank forest floor. Crickets chirped. The leaves rustled. I tried to sit up, but found that I was pinned down by something unseen. I could move my legs and head, but not my arms. I could not pick myself up.

Nervous, I craned my neck to look at the tree looming above. There, descending the branches was a long brown snake. Its forked tongue flicked from its scaly jaw. It bared its teeth. It slithered toward me.

I struggled to get up, to run, but I was rooted there on the forest floor. Something held me fast. The snake descended.

I felt a hard squeeze on my left breast. I heard a familiar moan in my ear.

Slowly, I realized that this was no dream. My eyes peeled open, and I tried to sit. But here I found that I was held pinned to my cot. All I could see was the dark wall before me. Someone was behind me. I felt flesh and sweat and heat. Someone breathed on my neck. Something hard rubbed and pushed at my thighs.

I froze.

The moaning deepened.

I drew a breath to scream, but a hand clamped over my lips.

"Shh, my little sister," hissed a voice. "Don't be scared. It's me. Brother Sanaa."

I squirmed and freed my arms, pushing myself up. But he grappled with me and threw me back down onto the cot.

"My little sister, don't be scared. I'm not gonna hurt you."

Again, I tried to scream. Again, he clamped his hand over me. He pushed his weight over my shoulder, his face bearing down on mine. Even in the darkness, I could make out the red paint on his nose and cheeks, the eyeliner framing his black eyes.

"I thought you might be frightened sleeping in this big room all by yourself." He moaned, the hard thing pressing up to me again. "That's why I'm here in your bed. To give you company."

Sanaa struggled with me, groping at my breast, thrusting against me.

My breath came in shallow, terrified bursts. My throat welled up. My mind screamed, but my voice would not come. I prayed for intervention. But all I could do was listen and lay.

The door squeaked open. The clown froze. I wrenched my forehead away from Sanaa's sweaty hand and looked up toward the doorway. Bright light poured in from the hallway. My guardian stood in its yellow relief. My guardian seemed to look at me for a time, but her eyes must have strained against the darkness, for she simply walked passed and went straight to her bed. Another woman followed. This one I couldn't make out, but she said something softly to my guardian and then found her own bed.

Sanaa shushed me. He held one hand fast over my lips. He moaned so softly that only I could hear.

My fear was replaced immediately by crippling embarrassment. I cried, but I did so quietly, because I didn't want to wake the others. I curled into a ball, once again facing the wall. I lay in this way, tears streaming over my cheeks, until morning.

—⟨∞⟩—

I rolled over at the nudge on my shoulder. I was greeted by the soft, smiling face of my guardian.

"Time to wake," she said.

I wiped my nose with the back of my hand, tried to hide that I'd been crying. Concern crept over my guardian's face for a moment, but then flickered away. I wanted to tell her, but I feared that no one would believe me. Sanaa was perhaps the most respected member of the group. Accusing him without proof would likely get me into trouble.

The rest of the tour was like a waking dream. I prayed day and night for it to end soon so I could get home to see my mother and sister.

Finally the day came when we would board the plane for Ulaanbaatar. I ran to the bus, willing it to get home quickly. I cried. When the bus found my stop, I tore down the aisle and sprinted home, dragging my bag in the snow behind me.

I rushed through the gate, up the walk, and into my ger. There, I found

Mom watching the television I had purchased for the family. She looked back at me with a grand smile.

"You're home already!" she said pleasantly.

I wanted desperately to break down, fall into my mother's arms, tell her about Sanaa, but when I saw her delighted face, I couldn't go through with it. Mom hugged me and kissed my cheek. She cradled me for a moment. She cooed over my head. I felt like a child again. I held my secret inside.

At work over the weeks to follow, Sanaa grew bolder and more comfortable in his approach to me. In very short order, he seemed to devise a strategy on where, when, and how he could get close to me. I tried to avoid him, but he always seemed to be lurking wherever I turned. Many times, I thought about telling someone of my torment, but I never summoned the courage.

I have pored over this troubling portion of my life many times. I try to imagine myself in that situation if I had known then what I know now. The truth is, I'm not sure I could have done anything differently. Beyond the pain and the embarrassment, beyond the fear of getting into trouble, I had the political strife to consider. This was a Socialist country under Communist rule. Even if I were to tell an adult, and even if I could manage to find verifiable proof, no one would have believed me. I was just a child, after all. I would be branded a liar and a deviant—someone trying to disrupt a reputable man's good family. I would be shamed, and so would my mother.

Never mind that elders were always held as correct and children always held as liars, Sanaa was also a respected and senior member of the circus. The fact that he was married with children didn't help, either. Here was an honorable man, a good guy, a paragon of the neighborhood.

And here was my tormentor.

CHAPTER 8

Keeping a secret like mine is torture. It is a pain that is only exacerbated by going to work every day and seeing the tormentor's face. Sanaa's glances and advances were bad enough. Having to walk around and pretend like nothing had happened was the true horror.

I would find myself alone in a darkened corner with the clown, pinned against two walls while he moaned and leered. I would quiver and cower. And when he would finally leave me, I would topple to my knees and pray.

I did a great deal of praying in those days. It was the only way that I could ever catch my breath after one of our terrifying encounters. I would pray after Sanaa left. I would pray after Norovsambuu yelled at me. I would pray when I noticed that my body had gotten fuller and the producers began calling me fat.

No matter how often I prayed, I always made sure to do it in private. Despite my pain, I never showed emotion to anyone.

"You never show emotion!" Norovsambuu would yell after a particularly dull performance in practice. "Why are you like that?"

I would just shrug and shake my head.

——⟨⟨∽⟩⟩——

Later that winter, I would get my first reprieve from Sanaa, and also my first taste of fame. I was selected to travel on a second countryside tour, this time with a much smaller ensemble. Among them were the famous singers Adarsuren, Nandintsetseg, and Siilegmaa. The other member of the Xyzgaareen Tsergeen Ensemble was an accordionist named Mr. Olzii. Apart from the musicians, there was only me. So I would be the visual highlight of the show, the only physical performer onstage.

For forty-five days, we would all get from town to town in a small, Jeep-like car called a 69. The Russian-made rumbler had a canvass top and not nearly enough seating for the five performers and their equipment. Still, we somehow managed to cram ourselves inside.

From the moment we left Ulaanbaatar, I could tell that this would be a much nicer tour than my last. Not only would Sanaa not be present, but my fellow performers proved to be abundantly pleasant. Ms. Nandintsetseg and Ms. Siilegmaa immediately took a shine to me, mothering over me as if I were their own daughter.

At our first hotel, I admitted to my newfound fear of sleeping alone, so Ms. Siilegmaa told me that I could sleep in her bed with her. From that point onward, she and I were like sisters. In fact, given that we both had rather round faces, people used to ask us all the time if we were sisters. So I had my sleeping partner and I had my new friend, Nandintsetseg, who always smelled of expensive perfume. It felt strange to be so close to a group of people who were essentially the superstars of Mongolian music at the time.

We would travel from small town to small town, and many people would already be waiting for us at our hotel. Crowds would line up, hoping to catch a glimpse of the famous Mr. Adarsuren or the famous Nandintsetseg. Children would push to get to the front, reaching out to touch the jackets of the icons passing by.

No one from the crowds ever called out my name, but I still felt special to be walking in tow with these people. Really, it was my first brush with the concept of fame, and I found myself reveling in the feeling. We slept in deluxe rooms, ate the finest foods, played before large, quiet crowds. When the group would finish singing, the crowds would leap to their feet and clap so loudly and for so long that they would be forced to remain onstage. Our programs were supposed to be forty-five minutes to an hour, but we would always end up performing for nearly two hours. Even I, as steely as I was, would cry at times as I performed.

After blowing away the crowds at bandbox theaters like the Sumiin Club, we would spend an evening at dinner with either Mr. Olzii or some family or another who invited us into their home. We would always leave at sunrise to head for the next town.

One morning, we woke with the sun to find clouds gathered overhead. Mr. Olzii said it looked like snow, but he still wanted to press on to our next engagement.

A few hours into our journey, the snow began to fall. It fell softly at first, but soon grew to a torrent the likes of which I had never seen. The blizzard came in sheets. I rubbed my hand over the frosted rear window of the 69, and all I could see in any direction was white.

Ms. Nandintsetseg and Ms. Siilegmaa began bickering with Mr. Olzii, who kept waving at the road as if dismissing it out of hand. Mr. Adarsuren maintained a heady silence. I shivered and worried.

A muffled thud hit the hood of the 69, and we all lurched forward. Our car had been brought to a sudden halt. Mr. Olzii cursed as he swung his door open and stepped out of the cab and out of sight. The singers and I piled out of the car, two per side. I was the last to slide into the cold. I plodded through the snow, already ankle-deep, to the front of the car, where I saw that we had collided with a prodigious snow bank.

Mr. Olzii grunted.

"No sense in getting all worked up," Mr. Adarsuren said softly. "We'll just have to push."

Mr. Olzii grunted again.

"Well, then," Mr. Adarsuren said, turning to us. "You and the other ladies can sit in the car. We'll need someone to steer us away from the bank, anyway. The men will push."

I grinned up at Ms. Nandintsetseg, sensing that she had no desire to sit idly in the car. She fired a hot breath through her nose and rubbed her bare hands together, readying herself for work. So the lot of us moved around to the front of the car, our legs buried to the thighs in the snow. We pushed with all our might. The wheels struggled against the icy road, buried too deep in the surrounding snow to budge.

We all began to shiver. I crossed my arms over my chest and held my hands under them. I was dressed for cold, but not this level of cold. My shoes were soaking wet already, and my toes had begun to numb.

"We have to dig," Mr. Olzii said—to the snow itself more than to any of us.

Reflexively, we all plunged into the snow bank, kicking up snow in small handfuls and tossing it onto the level ground beside the car.

The snow continued to fall. Apart from our strained breathing as we beat at the relentless snow bank, silence ruled the moment. As I took a break from my shoveling, I realized for the first time that there was no one else on this road. We were stranded out here in the middle of nowhere, and there would be no one likely to come along to help us anytime soon. A strange sort of desperation came over me. I dropped down and began to shovel with a renewed fervor.

The snow kept falling.

We were all dressed warmly, but our clothes were no match for the unyielding snow and heavy winds. The snow blew in such thick sheets that it was often difficult for me to see Ms. Nandintsetseg, though she worked right beside me.

We began taking turns sitting in the relative warmth of the car. But by the time the first hour had passed, the heat trapped in the cabin had long evaporated. I had never been so cold in all my young life. The snow kept falling. Help would not come. And we were stuck here. Fear overwhelmed me. I sat down in the snow.

We're gonna die here, I thought. A tear rolled down my cheek, freezing in place near my lips.

After a time, Ms. Nandintsetseg noticed that I wasn't helping anymore and sat down beside me. She passed her bare and blue hand up and down over my back, warming me some.

"There, there, dear," she said. "We'll get out of this yet. It can't snow forever."

As if it was taking a cue from her, the storm let up some. The snow fell now in casual flakes, not in the torrent of white from before.

Mr. Olzii went to the trunk of the 69 and removed a set of blankets to distribute to the women. The men then held a long, shifty conversation behind the trunk of the car. Through chattering teeth, I asked Ms. Nandintsetseg what they were discussing, but she offered only a shivering shrug.

Finally, the men stopped their hushed but frantic talk and began walking down the road away from the car.

"We're going to walk a little ways back to see if we can find anyone who lives nearby," Mr. Adarsuren called to us.

"Oh no!" Ms. Siilegmaa protested with a furrowed brow. "You shouldn't go anywhere."

Ms. Nandinsetseg nodded in agreement as she pulled me closer to her, wrapping our blanket tighter around us.

"We aren't going to go far," Mr. Adarsuren insisted. "Just a little ways down the road."

Before any of us could protest further, Mr. Adarsuren took off after Mr. Olzii, his steps wide and awkward from the snow. I watched the men trudge away from us until they were out of sight, swallowed up by the snow.

I nuzzled against Ms. Nandinsetseg. Ms. Siilegmaa's cheeks were a cherry red. She rocked back and forth on her haunches, a brown woolen blanket wrapped around her. Like it or not, we would be rooted here, clinging to our last vestiges of warmth until the men returned.

Every minute that passed felt like ten. Every ten minutes felt like an hour. It was perhaps an hour later when we heard our first noise. My heart leapt when I realized it was a car. It leapt again when the window rolled down, revealing that Mr. Olzii rode in the passenger seat.

"They've offered to take us back to the locals," he said. "Someone's going to put us up for the night."

We were all too cold to cheer, but I felt it in my heart. It came in great waves of relief—that same feeling a person gets when her head finally meets the pillow after an especially trying day.

It wasn't far to the nearest farmer's home. As soon as we entered, the people who lived there welcomed us as if we were family. They gave us hot tea. The lady of the house cooked hot food for us. I was so cold that I had trouble clasping my hands around my teacup. The food brought a kind of joyful warmth to me that spread from within. When we first arrived, I couldn't stop shivering. By the time the meal had ended, I was about as content as I can ever remember being.

That night, in a show of appreciation to our hosts, we staged a small performance for them. The famous singers belted their song while I contorted my body as best I could. I was sore from the cold and exhausted, but I think the show went well.

The following morning, Mr. Olzii went with the man of the house to fetch our car while the rest of us caught a ride into town to begin rehearsing for our concert. I felt much better on this day, but that feeling wouldn't last. Less than a week after our brush with the blizzard, I came down with a terrible throat infection and fever. Mr. Olzii started me on antibiotics, but things only worsened. In time, it was all I could do to breathe, let alone perform. The fever had drained me such that I could scarcely keep my eyes open for longer than a few minutes at a time. I slept most of the day and night.

"You know," I heard Ms. Nandinsetseg say to Mr. Olzii—the two of them were standing over my bed, apparently unaware that I was still awake. "I heard that wolf's tongue helps in cases like this."

"Wolf's tongue?" Mr. Olzii asked, sounding incredulous.

Ms. Nandintsetseg looked down at me. Just beneath my heavy eyelids, I could see the deep concern spread across her face.

"Yes," she said. "But it has to be warm."

Mr. Olzii scoffed. "Where in the world are you going to find wolf's tongue?"

"I have my ways."

I spent the remainder of the day inanimate. My body felt as if it were on fire. I couldn't move. I could hardly breathe. I passed in and out of consciousness for much of the afternoon.

Eventually, I pried open my eyes to see Ms. Nandinsetseg stagger up to my bed. She held a paper bag in her left hand, and it swayed back and forth under her unsteady grip. I could see that she was drunk. When she knelt down beside me and began to speak, my theory was confirmed by the liquor I could smell on her breath.

"I got it," she said, lurching forward to lean over me. "Let's get this over with."

I turned my head away. A cold, moist sensation crept over the front of my neck. I fell asleep with that slimy, smelly thing leeched to my throat.

When I woke later that night, I was surprised to find that I could breathe without laboring. By morning, I did indeed feel much better—well enough to sit up and even eat some soup brought to me by Ms. Siilegmaa.

Ms. Nandinsetseg never revealed how and where she got the wolf's tongue, but I found myself not caring. As bad as things had been for me, it was entirely possible that Ms. Nandinsetseg had saved my life. And she did it with such kindness and selflessness that I can't imagine a more wonderful human being.

For a full three months after my return from the solo tour with the musicians, Uugii and I had our dressing room all to ourselves. This was because Norovsambuu had been called away to tour overseas. This left the two of us with the run of the place. And Uugii being the kind of mischief maker that she was, it was only a matter of time before we got ourselves into trouble.

We performed the finale for the local show that fall, so life became a little more stable than usual. Uugii and I would usually retreat to our dressing room together following our responsibility to the show, then return to watch the finish from the audience. But on one of the days in late November, I had a friend come in to watch us perform, so I went down to the audience to speak to her before I even changed. We spoke only briefly, as my friend wanted to get back to watching the show, so I headed back to the dressing room to change.

When I arrived, I found Uugii lounging in her chair with two young men at her feet. The men, who were acrobats that I knew, were sitting cross-legged on the floor, each of them smoking a cigarette. I was so startled to see men in our room that it took me a moment to realize that they were smoking in our dressing room and that this might not be the greatest idea. Smoking was certainly common in Mongolia in those days, but not for people as young as we were.

Of course it only took one of her famous puckish expressions for Uugii to get me to ignore that we were breaking the rules and sit down with her. We all enjoyed a short conversation while they finished their cigarettes. We were careful to blow the smoke out the small window between Uugii's and my vanities. In time, they left.

Uugii and I passed the next few minutes gossiping about the boys. Uugii was smitten with one of them, and she wanted to know whether I thought the feeling was mutual. Neither of us realized that the room still reeked of smoke. Neither of us heard the door to our dressing room open.

"What is going on?" came a familiar voice.

Uugii and I turned our attention to the doorway. There, just inside the hall, stood Tsetsgee, another contortionist.

"You're *smoking* in here?" she barked.

With another of her famous grins, Uugii shrugged. "Surely you don't mean *us*."

I winced. Tsetsgee's face burned red.

"You girls are too young to be smoking!" she hollered. "This is bad! Bad!"

"But we didn't—" I tried to say, but Tsetsgee had already stormed out.

Uugii laughed girlishly, but I didn't share her amusement. Something told me that this wouldn't be the last we would hear from Tsetsgee on this matter. I had a feeling that we would be in big trouble.

When we were called, we went out to perform the final bow before the audience. We danced and carried on for the post-show performance. And when it was over, we returned to our dressing room. There, we were met by a thoroughly bureaucratic-looking fellow performer standing in our door.

"Hello," she said haughtily. She scrunched her narrow nose. "The director of the Women's Group would like a word with you."

Uugii and I exchanged a worried glance and then nodded. We followed the woman down the hall and into a dressing room. There, we were met by five or six other women, all of them already seated. There was no place for us to sit, so we stood in the middle of the circle they had formed. We did so hesitantly, feeling a little like victims of the Inquisition.

The woman we knew to act as director of the group cleared her throat. "Okay, then. Tell us why you were smoking in your dressing room."

We both stared at the floor, saying nothing.

"Whose idea was it?" the director demanded.

We kept staring. Every second that passed in silence was agonizing. I heard the director draw another angry breath to chide us, but Uugii finally spoke up.

"It wasn't us," she said.

"But who could it have been?" the director demanded. "It was only the two of you in the room."

Uugii shrugged. I felt like speaking out in our defense, but I knew there was no graceful way out of this—or at least, there was no way out of this that didn't involve us getting yelled at. I had learned enough in my few years as a traveling contortionist to know that the yelling would be less severe if we just kept our mouths shut.

"Tsetsgee," the director said, "what did you see?"

I turned to the left, noticing for the first time that Tsetsgee was one of the women assembled in the room. I felt a sudden but ridiculous sense of relief that we would at least be allowed to face our accuser.

Tsetsgee's expression was that of blinding derision. "I was walking down the hallway, and when I passed their room, I could smell smoke."

"So you went inside?"

Tsetsgee nodded with vigor. "I found *these two* smoking!"

I wanted to scream that it was a lie, but I couldn't—not if I wanted to escape the room without getting slapped.

The director turned her attention back to us, looking more satisfied than a woman in her position really ought. "So you two were caught smoking in your coach's dressing room while she was away."

My heart sank. I heard Uugii sniffle.

"There was a witness, and her account seems unassailable."

I stared at the floor again, hating the silence that followed.

"So here we have to decide what kind of punishment you will receive," the director said finally.

She passed the proverbial baton around the room, asking each woman present to offer a suggestion on what might pass as suitable punishment in a case such as this. The way they were talking, I felt almost like we had committed the crime of the century—as if smoking in a dressing room were the most unprecedented and heinous offense a young girl could ever commit.

Finally, a consensus was reached.

"We're all agreed, then," the director said.

Every head, save for mine and Uugii's, nodded.

"Very well," the director said. "Girls, since you have chosen to act so unprofessionally in the absence of your esteemed coach, you have each been demoted to the role of supporting artist. Your pay will be reduced accordingly."

We left the room devastated. We returned to our own dressing room, dripping with tears. We had only just become professional artists. And now here we were being docked, moved back to the end of the line. Not only would our reputations and opportunities as performers suffer, but our salaries would be cut in half, as well.

The next month saw Uugii and me performing the best we could as supporting artists. It was difficult going from a high rank to a lower one. The truth was that despite our occasional mischief making, Uugii and I had learned a great deal under the tutelage of our legendary coach. To be performing as supporting artists was more than just a modest slight.

When the month had ended, our coach finally returned. The moment she saw the docket for the upcoming tour, she asked why Uugii and I had been listed as supporting artists. We explained to her what had happened. With a look of grave anger, Norovsambuu departed.

An hour later, she returned to the dressing room, expressionless as usual.

"You're back to being professional artists," she said simply.

Uugii and I squealed with delight, tumbling into an excited hug.

"Don't take this for granted," Norovsambuu warned. "You have to use your heads while I'm away."

Our excitement died in a moment. We stood and nodded solemnly, each of us thanking Norovsambuu in a somber fashion that didn't match the joy in our hearts. We had been wrongly accused of a minor crime and punished severely for it. But that was life as a performer in those days: sometimes, you faced tremendous hardship. Sometimes, you were punished for things you didn't deserve to be punished for. And sometimes, you were rewarded simply because your friends were so esteemed.

CHAPTER 9

Around that time, all my friends at school began to take an interest in boys. It wouldn't be long before many of them had boyfriends. I might have joined them, except that every time I thought about boys, my heart began beating so quickly I could hardly breathe. Maybe it was my sheltered young life. Maybe it was the fact that my only male role model had died when I was still very young. Maybe it was what Sanaa had done to me. Or maybe I've always just been painfully shy.

Whatever the case, I didn't have a particularly good relationship with the boys in my class—or even the men at the circus.

Looking back, I think that might be why Norovsambuu first suggested sending me to Circus College to take ballet classes. Sure, the classes would help broaden my horizons and improve me as a performer, but I suspect now that my coach sent me away to school to try and help me open up a little. I wasn't a hermit by any stretch of the imagination, but there was no denying that there were only two people outside of my home that I ever spoke to: Uugii and Norovsambuu. My coach must have seen that I couldn't continue on like this or I would be socially awkward for the rest of my life. And that wouldn't do—not backstage and not onstage. Nobody wanted to work with a performer who shied away from all conversation, and nobody wanted to watch a performer who couldn't properly emote.

So I went away to Circus College. There, on the very first day, I met a nice girl named Oyunchuluun, who everyone called Oyunaa.

Oyunaa was rather plain as girls go, but there was a kindness in her eyes unlike anything I had ever seen. She accepted me with such warmth that it was difficult not to love and identify with her from the very beginning. She introduced me around the class, and I found myself smiling and talking to everyone I met.

I think what made me so comfortable was the fact that everyone in my class was close to my age. This would be the first time in my life that I would be involved with an artistic endeavor that didn't include men and women of all ages, after all.

Oyunaa and I clicked right from the start. We spent a great deal of time together at school, and even some time together at home. As it turned out, she lived right across the street from my ger, so the coincidence would lead us to be fast friends at home as well.

When I was first introduced to Oyunaa's parents, I could tell that they liked me. I was much like their daughter, after all—both of us quiet and unassuming. And yet, whenever Oyunaa and I were together, we brought out a great spontaneity and zest for life in each other.

I respected Oyunaa for her patience. But more than anything, I respected her for never looking down on me because I came from a poor family.

The two of us would walk home together from Circus College every day that I had my ballet class, and our conversations would often be so dynamic and animated that I could hardly believe we had reached our street already. On weekends when I wasn't performing, we would go all over the capital to see different shows—ballets, operas, live concerts.

Whenever I had time, I attended concert school at the Od Kino Theater, as it was called, which was quite close to my home. Here, I met another young girl who would become a close friend.

Tsenge was about my age, and maybe two inches taller than me. She had short, light-brown hair and was pale skinned. With her slender body and long legs, she was quite fetching, and whenever she batted her big, brown eyes at the boys, they tended to take interest. It helped that she was one of the more outgoing and talkative girls I had ever known, of course. She was quite funny and as sweet as anyone I had ever met. This meant that she had many friends, but for whatever reason, she liked to spend most of her time with me. And the feeling was mutual. Whenever I wasn't with Oyunaa, there was a good chance you would find me with Tsenge.

I remember the first time she invited me over to her house. It was far away from my ger, the apartment building in which she lived, and I mean that in both the sense of location and economic status. Hers was a fine, Russian-built apartment complex, one of many in the city that was nine stories high. Tsenge's family lived on the fifth floor in a lovely two-bedroom apartment that was rather cramped for her family of two parents and eight children. Of course, some of the kids had moved out, having grown up and taken wives or husbands of their own, but that still didn't leave much room for Tsenge, her brother and three sisters, and their parents.

There was not a whole lot of furniture in the house—which was common in those days—but what they did have was quite nice. The parents slept in the living room, which was well outfitted with a sofa, small table, television, and a pair of plush chairs. The kitchen had a stove and a new refrigerator, along with a table for serving dinner. Each bedroom was equipped with a pair of soft and comfortable beds, nightstands, and dressers. The bathroom had a shower, which was a luxury in those days.

I was intimidated by the relative opulence of my new friend's home, but whatever trepidation I held was quickly put at ease by Tsenge's mother. Tsenge looked like her mother, I noticed immediately. Both were tall, had excellent bone structure, and big eyes. By contrast, Tsenge's father was shorter than his wife and darker skinned. They were an older couple, but quick to make me feel at home.

Tsenge's mother beamed down at me with a motherly expression I had never experienced outside my own home.

"Could you do your act for us?" she asked me timidly.

"Of course!" I said respectfully. I then got down on the floor and began my latest routine.

When I finished, I stood to a healthy round of applause. It filled me with a joy equal to the applause I would receive onstage. That has always been something that has fascinated me: it doesn't matter where the applause comes from or what size the crowd; it always feels the same.

Tsenge's family loved the performance so much that it became a recurring theme that I would have to perform my latest act whenever I came over to Tsenge's. Many times, this meant performing the same act on consecutive days, but her family never seemed to mind.

Unfortunately, my friendship with Tsenge would be short lived, as Tsenge was chosen to attend school in the Czech Republic only a month after we met. In my sadness, her older sister, Hombi, took me under her wing, and we became fast friends.

While it was nice to be making so many new friends, Hombi was probably my first friend who made me feel inferior in terms of beauty. She was a cheerful, outgoing girl, two years my senior, and remarkably beautiful. Every party in town seemed to have an invitation for her, and as her friend, I would usually go along. Boys always paid plenty of attention to Hombi, but never any attention to me. Not one boy liked me. At the time, I wasn't sure how to feel about that fact. On the one hand, it was disheartening to know that I paled in comparison to my new friend. On the other, it was nice not to have to deal with all the stresses and heartbreaks that I watched Hombi endure. With school, learning new contortions, learning new routines, providing for my family, and managing my increasingly busy social life, I had enough on my plate as it was, after all.

It wasn't necessarily that I was ugly. I was just awkward. From the time I entered my teens, I was an especially curvy young girl. And when you get curves that early, it often comes with its share of chubbiness. For the longest time, many at the Circus College would call me fat and ugly. It wasn't long before this contributed to a rather crippling depression. If not for Oyunaa and Hombi, I might not have made it through. I trusted them with everything, nearly. They would comfort me when I was feeling lonely or scorned. They would give me hope whenever I felt as if there was nothing I could do to overcome the torment. And they would always be there to listen to anything I had to say.

Looking back, my only wish is that I would have had the courage to share with them what had happened with Sanaa the Clown. If I had, maybe I would have healed before the torment had a chance to take root. But no matter how badly I wanted to tell one of my friends about that horrible time in my life—and I came close to telling Oyunaa once or twice—I could never overcome the shame.

Anyway, despite my dark secret, Hombi and I quickly became best friends. A summer would pass, and I would reach high school age. My school was close to Hombi's family's apartment, so I would always go straight over to her place after school. Sometimes, her family would be there; sometimes they would come later. I remember one such day when Hombi's mother entered the apartment and found us talking in the kitchen. She smiled and asked me a question I never thought I would hear.

"Oh, little Otgo," she said as she often did, "I was wondering, might I get a chance to meet your mother?"

Caught off-guard though I was, I eagerly agreed to the idea. Mother had lately made it a habit to incessantly question me about my whereabouts following school, and no matter how many times I told her I was just over at Hombi's, she never seemed to find quiet. I think she was just nervous that I was consorting with a less than honorable family. A long and happy visit from Hombi's mom two days later put an end to that.

Between Oyunaa and Hombi, I grew up with an unusual set of friends. Both of them were at least two years older than me, after all, so I got used to doing the things that an older girl might do. It wasn't what one might think. I actually found a nice balance between the two of them—Oyunaa being soft-hearted, caring, and patient, and Hombi being cheerful, outgoing, talented, and abundantly happy.

Not long after I entered high school, Hombi would finish her schooling and immediately go to work as an actress for the XZ theatre. We were all very excited, particularly when she landed the lead role in her first play, a drama called *Khaireeg Khairla.*

She was a nervous wreck every time she thought about carrying the whole show as the lead. One night, I was sleeping over at her house when I woke to the horrible sensation that someone was pulling my hair and yelling into my ear. When I gained full consciousness, I realized that Hombi had moved in behind me in bed and was indeed pulling my hair back into a pony tail. I felt a tightening sensation around the spot where she held it in place with her fingers, then the unmistakable sound of cutting.

I screamed and leapt to my feet. I ran to the door and switched on the light. When I turned back to the bed, I saw Hombi, muttering to herself with her eyes half-closed. She held a shiny pair of scissors in one hand and a huge swath of my hair in the other.

"Hombi," I said hesitantly.

She continued to mutter.

"Hombi!" I yelled.

She shook her head, her eyes fluttering open. "Wha-What?"

My eyes widened as I took my mangled hair in my hand and showed it to her. She looked down at what she held then. She questioned the scissors with her eyes, then ran her fingers through my lopped hair as if combing through fine linen.

"Oh my," she said. "Oh my God, Otgo. I'm so sorry."

With tears in my eyes, I went to the bathroom to examine the damage. There, staring back at me, I saw a tired, worried, wrecked version of myself. My first reaction was sorrow—the kind of sorrow I imagine might come with the loss of a limb. My long hair had always been a part of me, and now here it was gone. But then, the more I examined it, the more I began to like the way I looked with a bobbed cut.

In the mirror, I saw Hombi enter the bathroom. The exhausted sadness in her eyes lingered only long enough for her to take in my new look. She lit up with an energy so warm I could never fend it off, even if I wanted to.

"You look amazing!" she said.

I cracked a quick smile. I ran my fingers through the little hair I had left. I *did* look amazing.

"I should cut hair in my sleep more often," she said.

We both began to giggle, then to laugh, then to cackle. We carried on like this for several minutes, laughing at each other as I sashayed around, showing off and checking out every angle of my new and unexpected haircut.

A knock came softly against the door. Hombi attempted a somber look with her eyes, but we were both too giddy to mind much what awaited us outside the bathroom. With a giggle, she opened the door. There, as expected, stood her mother.

"What on earth is going on?" she said in a stage whisper. "It's the middle of the night. Why are you two laughing?"

Hombi shrugged and gazed over at me. I watched as her mother's eyes followed. All at once, her anger turned to confusion.

"What have you done to your hair, Otgo?"

Cackling anew, we took turns explaining to her what had happened.

"What on earth?" she repeated, glaring now at her daughter. "Are you going crazy or what?"

Hombi giggled. "I guess I've been rehearsing too much. I'm even starting to rehearse in my sleep."

At that, even Hombi's mom had to smile. But she didn't hold it long. "You're lucky it was just her hair. You could've killed her."

With everyone still ruffling with laughter, Hombi's mom escorted us down the hall and back into Hombi's room. There, the two of us tumbled into bed, still grinning and giggling and touching at my hair.

Not long after the haircut incident, I was scheduled to perform in one of my favorite annual performances. There was a question as to whether my hair would look presentable by the time the show began, but as I recall, things were fine.

In any case, my favorite performance of the year was held at the DCNKA building in Ulaanbaatar. The DCNKA was a building the Russians had built for themselves to serve as the Russian cultural center. Each year during the New Year celebration, they would have a series of circus performances for the local Russian schoolchildren. Kids would be bussed in from nearby cities to watch us perform. Then, afterward, they would throw a party for the children, complete with gift bags full of candies, fine chocolates, and small toys. We would do this several times per day, each time performing for a new busload of kids.

Of course the reason I liked this occasion was because I was allowed to attend the parties, being as young and as close to the action as I was. This meant that I would get access to the gift bags several times each day. I would enjoy one for myself and then take as many as I could to give as gifts to my family and friends.

The year of my unplanned haircut was a good one for me. The Russians fed us quite well with their favored cuisine, and I managed to make off with several bags of goodies.

CHAPTER 10

Because I started working at a young age, I didn't have time for many of the things that most young girls get to experience. While most little girls worry only about pleasing their parents and getting the various inconsequential things that they want, I had to worry about pleasing a whole host of people and was always far too busy for wanting, let alone getting. That group of people began, of course, with my mother, but was followed closely by the director and producer of the State Circus.

What made this fact more difficult was that the State Circus often changed their directors and producers. For the performers, these two people were the most important people in their professional lives. Having to consistently learn to appease new people was a challenge for me.

I learned early on that some producers wanted a suck-up. Others wanted nothing but hard work. Some knew my name. Others could care less. Some appreciated my talents. Others did not. And depending on who wielded the keys to the building and the upcoming performances, I would get paid more or less money and would be chosen more or less often to go overseas to perform major roles on the big stage.

By the time I turned fifteen, we had our latest new producer, a stark man named Mandakh. His dark eyes always seemed to be on me, and they never held favor. At the time, I was quite strong, even for my age, but I was also chubby, thickly built, fat.

"You are no performer," Mandakh would say. "Look at you! Why would any audience ever *want* to look at you?"

It was a harsh truth, one that a fifteen-year-old girl isn't normally equipped to manage. A fifteen-year-old girl leading a normal life might cry to her mother or her friend about how harshly her new teacher was treating her. She might be told to ignore the barbs and just be the woman she was meant to be. But for me, there was a different reality to face. I lived in Socialist Mongolia. The Party simply didn't allow performers on stage who were anything but skinny. Ballerinas, circus performers, dancers—all of them were rail-thin.

Every day, the coaches under Mandakh's regime would call me fat. After every meeting, Mandakh himself would hand me a special note telling me to lose weight. Eventually, when it became clear that no matter what I tried, I wasn't going to slim down fast enough for Mandakh, he would call me out in front of the other performers and coaches whenever the subject of health and wellness came up.

"For example!" he would yell to anyone who would listen. "Contortionist Otgontsetseg. She is so very fat. She needs to lose weight." Then he would level his awful eyes on me as I tried to make myself as invisible as possible in a room full of people. "She knows that if she doesn't lose weight, we will not let her perform on the big stage."

Whenever called out in this way, I would shrink in my seat and feel my face turn red. It always left me wanting to crawl into a hole.

Because of my weight issues, Mandakh would only send me on the countryside traveling show, a show that might have seemed beneath me, considering some of the places I had been to by that point. But the countryside show was always my favorite, so I didn't complain. Thirty to forty-five days of traveling around my own beautiful country—I still felt blessed even where I might have felt slighted. The only complaint I could possibly lodge was that I would have to travel for thirty to forty-five days, come home, spend a few days with my mother—just long enough for her to clean my clothes and repack my bags—and then have to turn around and do the whole tour again. I began to miss my mother, my sisters, and my friends, but I knew that I had no choice but to just accept the fact that things would be this way until I learned to please my new producer.

Fortunately, Mongolia is the most beautiful country in the world, so I had plenty to look at whenever I went on a tour. And whenever I felt like complaining about the lot I had drawn, I would remind myself that I was getting paid a fair amount of money to do exactly what I loved and dreamed of doing.

"Sometimes things get tough," Mom would tell me. "Sometimes life seems too difficult to bear. But doing something you are good at, something that you love from the bottom of your heart—that is a treasure beyond all treasures. I know it doesn't look like it now, my little girl, but someday this will all bring you true happiness."

I still remember everything she said, just as if she had spoken the words to me yesterday.

Each year, every performer at the Mongolian Circus would have to pass a professional performer's test. For the test, everyone would have to complete a number of tasks before a panel that included the director, producer, artistic director, and the many coaches. The first was their latest act. For the second, the test taker would have to juggle at least three balls, clubs, or rings. Third would be walking the low-wire. Fourth was an acrobatic maneuver of the test taker's choosing. And finally, the test taker would have to answer a number of questions about the history of the Mongolian Circus.

Passing the test was essential to anyone who wanted to remain employed by the circus, but there was also a bonus. If your score was high enough, you would be paid as a top-tier performer. This right would be passed to those who achieved the four or five top test scores. The next four or five from the top would receive a pay raise from their current salary. Everyone else would remain in their same pay group as when they had started.

For those who performed less than ideally, a note would arrive from the judges, explaining what could have been done better. For those who failed the test, there would be unemployment—or, in the event that the performer was well-liked or just plain lucky, the position would be retained at severely reduced pay.

Having spent a hard year on the road, touring the countryside, my professional performer's test at the age of sixteen went quite well. I passed all my five elements with flying colors. And yet, when I went to check on my pay raise, I found that I had not received one. I didn't even have to question the judges directly, for they had included a special note in the packet explaining my scores and pay grade: I was too fat for a raise.

Later, I would find out that every other contortionist in the circus would receive more money that year. But for fat Otgo, there would be no extra money. And for fat Otgo, there would be another two years relegated to the countryside.

Several months after my test, I returned home from my latest tour. Upon visiting the dressing room I still shared with Norovsambuu, I found a note waiting for me from Mandakh. It asked for my immediate presence, along with Norovsambuu, in the producer's office. If I had had a tail, it would have been tucked between my legs as I made the long, slow walk down the hall with my coach.

Together, we entered a room I had visited many times, never happily since the hiring of Mandakh. My least favorite producer glared at me from over his military-straight desk. Norovsambuu and I sat in the chairs he waved toward. Mandakh didn't waste any time.

"Otgo is very fat," he said pointedly. "And for that, I'm gonna give her a *Tsagaan Khuudas*."

I slumped at the shoulders, having eyes only for my hands. A Tsagaan Khuudas is an especially damning note to receive.

"If she doesn't lose weight in three months, I will exercise the Tsagaan Khuudas, and Otgo will be fired."

Norovsambuu nodded solemnly. I did my level best not to cry.

"Starting today, Otgo will be bumped down to supporting artist. Her check will be halved."

I let out a little whimper. Norovsambuu burned me with her eyes. As much as I hated Mandakh in that moment, my respect for my coach—and my constant desire not to upset her—won out. I buried my tears and nodded faithfully.

"That is all," Mandakh said.

My head feeling heavy, I lumbered to my feet. As I waited for my coach to stand and lead me out, I did the math in my head. When I first entered the office, I had been making T300. And now, upon being excused, I would be making T150.

"Please don't cut her paycheck," Norovsambuu said.

My heart leapt. My coach was standing up for me. Tears returned to my eyes.

"What did you say?" Mandakh asked, his round head cocking to one side in exaggerated disbelief.

"Her family is very poor."

I watched as Mandakh's face reddened.

"Her mother is an old woman," Norovsambuu continued.

The producer seemed to be holding his breath, ready to explode.

"Please, just think about what this pay cut would do to her mother."

At that, Mandakh lost it. "I'm not taking any excuses!" he growled. "That's her life, not mine."

Norovsambuu stood, looking defeated. The two of us shuffled out of the room.

"If she's so poor, how can she be so fat?" Mandakh called behind us.

The question hit me like a blow to the back of the head. I tumbled into Norovsambuu, who carried me like an injured girl to our dressing room.

There, she sat me down, and with a light tone more motherly than I had ever seen in her, cooed softly that everything would be all right.

"You have to lose weight," she said to me. "But this time, I will help you."

I nodded, the tears flowing freely now.

"We'll start tomorrow."

I looked at her as if I was begging for my life. To my surprise, she appeared worried too.

When I had calmed some, the two of us changed out of our practice gear and into our street clothes. I would now have to go home and explain everything to my mother. The very thought was devastating. I didn't know how I could possibly tell her such terrible news. I never wanted disappoint my mother, but this would be especially crippling. I wanted only to make her proud of me, but now I would have to explain to her that my weight might get me fired.

To my surprise, Mother took the news that evening like she might take the newspaper. She nodded and harrumphed, then moved on to other topics. Not until the next morning did she really comment on the matter.

"Well, you'll just have to lose the weight," she said simply. "I don't want you to get fired."

I drew a breath to protest—to shout about how unfair Mandakh was being—but Mom cut me off.

"You have so much talent, Otgo," she said. "It would be a shame to lose your job over something so trivial."

Of course my mother meant to speak these words in the kindest of ways. She meant them as a comfort, but I couldn't help but take them as another blow to my fragile psyche. Disappointment doesn't even begin to describe how I felt in that moment. I knew a sadness utterly heart-wrenching.

For weeks, I couldn't sleep. I couldn't eat. All I could do was think about losing the weight so I could continue doing my shows. I didn't care if I would be relegated forever to traveling the countryside. I only wanted to get back to where my domineering new producer would allow me to perform at the pay I deserved.

Summer came. With no school to attend, I was able to train two times per day. In the morning, I would run laps at the circus and then run through my act ten times consecutively without stopping. For lunch, I would eat a small bowl of soup. Then, at night, I would jump rope, followed by two-hundred leaps up onto and then back down from a high chair.

The other performers would mean well whenever they gave me advice, but it would often feel an awful lot like teasing. In one such instance, I was approached by a couple of female performers a few years older than me.

"You should start having sex," one of them said.

"Oh yes," said the other. "Being sexually active gets the juices flowing."

"Helps you lose the weight quicker."

After a while, I started timing my practices, walks to the dressing room, and showers so I could avoid seeing any of the other performers. It was all just so embarrassing for me.

So I went into hiding, training in my dressing room instead of on the training floor. In this way, I trained harder than I have ever trained in my life. Two training sessions per day became three: morning, afternoon, and evening. I would train, take a shower, nap, and then wake up to train again. For two months, I trained in this way. There are racehorses that don't train as hard as I did. And in time, it paid off.

I stepped on the scale after the second month of training and saw the weights tip at ten whole kilograms fewer than when I had started. Norovsambuu smiled more broadly than I had ever seen her smile.

"Tomorrow, we will speak with Mandakh," she said.

I hopped off the scale, doing a happy little shake.

"But first," she said, "you have to write an *orgodol becheed*."

I nodded. This was a letter of pleading.

"Write something like, 'Please don't fire me. I believe that my training has shown my dedication to your honorable cause. Please reinstate my paycheck to its former level.'"

Word for word, I wrote everything my coach asked me to write.

The next morning, Norovsambuu and I went to Mandakh's office. He appeared surprised to see us, if only slightly annoyed.

"Otgo has trained very hard," Norovsambuu said, passing her hand in front of my body to show me off, "as you can see."

Mandakh cleared his throat in a haughty fashion.

"She lost a total of ten kilograms," Norovsambuu said. "And she has something she would like to share with you."

The producer offered an urgent wave. "Go ahead, then."

I straightened up and began to read the letter my coach had asked me to write.

When I had finished, Mandakh put his hand on his long, narrow chin and looked at me with wide eyes. "Okay, then." He was gruff. Terse. "Don't blow up like a fat balloon."

A month later, I was reinstated as a professional performer. By then, I had lost another six kilograms, bringing my total to sixteen. It was a massive relief for my mother and me to know that the money would be returning, but more than that, I felt like I had lifted a huge weight from my shoulders. Of course I literally *had* lifted a huge weight from my body, but I also felt happy again for the first time in years.

I learned a harsh lesson that year: you have to work for everything you get. It doesn't matter how talented you are if you're not willing to do what your superiors ask of you.

CHAPTER 11

I t was the spring of my sixteenth year. As was the case every spring, the government mandated that everyone must spend the season cleaning up their workplace and their neighborhood. This massive cleanup effort was called "Communist Subbotnick." I still smile when I think about fifty or sixty circus performers balancing inside and outside the State Circus building, cleaning windows, hosing down the big ring and the small ring, washing curtains, and pulling weeds. It was quite a sight.

The government often required us to do things outside our job description. For instance, one autumn, we were tasked to join the agricultural effort. All circus performers had to travel to a nearby town to help harvest the season's crops. It was quite cold that year, but for whatever reason, we left in the afternoon, arriving in the town at night.

Because it was so dark out and we were well outside the city, none of us could tell where we were upon exiting the bus. We all trundled in an unsteady line to the fields, where we would set up the few tents we had to house us for the night. When we finished, we all tumbled into our sleeping bags and passed out as soon as our heads hit our pillows.

The next morning, we were roused quite early—early even for a circus performer—and instructed on how to harvest our given crop. Some of us were assigned to pull potatoes. Others were assigned to pick cabbage. Regardless of assignment, the crop had to be pulled up by hand.

The first day we worked, within the first hour, it began to pour rain. It was cold, and the rain came down in sheets, and yet we had no choice but to continue working. We worked from sunrise to sunset, our only break coming at lunch. Of course, I was wildly and completely ill even before the day came to an end.

The next morning brought much of the same. More cold rain. On this day, we were to finish the harvest, but the rain delayed us terribly. I was so sick that I could hardly see. It was all I could do to finish work on the second day, and yet here I would still have another full day of required work.

On the first day of work, everyone was singing and laughing about the rain. But by the fourth day, when we were finally allowed to go home, nobody said a word. Sleep ruled the bus.

I ended up in bed for the week that would follow. Thank God for my mother. She took care of me better than any nurse could ever hope.

So that was the extracurricular life of a government performer.

By this time, I was still having trouble fending off Uugii's constant leadership. The two of us were sitting in one of Ulaanbaatar's few public saunas—her idea—and it had become too hot to bear.

"Let's get a drink," she said as we sat in the blinding steam.

"Okay," I said, and I stood to lead the way down the wooden steps.

The room was so hot that I could hardly see. And when my foot first met the slippery wood flooring, it failed me, and I fell. I dropped down the stair and landed on something sharp. When I rolled over, I saw that I had fallen onto a glass bottle, which had shattered and gashed my right kneecap. I cried out in pain. The few people in the sauna stared at me with open mouths. Only Uugii made a move to help me.

A throbbing ache erupted from my knee when Uugii pulled me to my feet. I looked down and saw that I was gushing blood. Tears began to spill down my face. Uugii pressed her hand to my wound to try and stop the bleeding, but the cut was too deep.

"I need to," I sputtered, "I need to go home."

"Not before we wrap this," Uugii said.

She turned and searched the sauna wildly for something that she could use. In the corner, she found, of all things, a plastic bag. She returned to me and wrapped the bag around my wound. Blood pulsed against the plastic, but for now it appeared that the makeshift bandage was doing the trick.

"How do we keep it in place?" I asked, my tears still flowing.

Kneeling, Uugii turned her head from side to side before settling on me. "Your headband. Give it to me."

I removed my elastic headband and handed it down to Uugii, who strung it over my ankle and pulled it up to my knee, where she wrapped it tightly around the bag. In this way, I could now walk with my bandage, but only slowly—and I would have to stop every few steps to straighten things out again.

It took a long while to get dressed and an even longer while to hobble to the bus stop, but with Uugii's help, I managed. She helped me pull my tights over my haphazard bandage, and she let me put my weight on her as we made our way down to the bus stop. I don't know if I would have made it were it not for my training partner.

Outside, the chill of early spring was still very much a factor. I shivered and shook as we waited for the bus. When mine arrived, I said my goodbyes and thank yous with Uugii, and then boarded and quickly found a seat. I did my best to remain inconspicuous through my pain and my pair of tights packed with plastic and blood, but it was difficult. An old woman with ratty gray hair stared at me almost the entire trip. I did what I could not to look at her. Her concern only would have made me start crying again.

Back at my ger, I pushed through the front door as quietly as I could.

But Mother was waiting for me. I practically bumped into her the moment I shuffled inside.

"What's wrong?" she said immediately, noticing that my face was pale and stricken. Then her eyes drifted down to my leg. "Oh my God!" she screamed. "What is this blood on your leg?"

I looked down and saw that I was bleeding through my tights.

"Take those off!" Mom said, her hands frantic and busy.

I pulled down my tights to reveal a bloody mass of plastic and skin. Mother howled in anguish. She cleaned my wound as best she could. I nearly lost consciousness when I looked down to see the cleaned cut. The bone was exposed. Mother kept scolding me, telling me that I had to be more careful, that I had a career to think about, to say nothing of my health.

When she finished, Mom scalded the wound with some medicine and then wrapped my leg with a proper bandage. She then told me to go straight to bed and sleep. I did as I was told.

In the middle of the night, I woke to searing pain. I clutched at my thigh. My knee throbbed. I wailed. Mother woke and came to comfort me. All through the night, this happened. I didn't get much sleep.

The next day, I stayed home from school and didn't go to training. All day, I was in tremendous pain.

By the second day, my pain was accompanied by dizziness and fever. Mother attended to me as best she could, but there was only so much she could do.

On the third day, my fever climbed so high that I began to talk like a crazy person. My right leg was fantastically swollen and dark red, and I was a jabbering madwoman.

Cooing for me to keep quiet, Mother carefully removed my bandage to check on my wound. And even in my troubled state, I could tell that it had become infected.

Mother rushed me to the bus stop, and together we went to the only hospital in the region with a trauma center—a big, long, two-story building of standard hospital white.

Not long after my arrival, I was laid up in a hospital bed, awaiting word from the doctor who had just inspected me.

"You should have brought her earlier," my doctor said to Mother. "It would have been easier to tend to her wound. But now she must stay for a few days."

"Is the infection bad?" Mom asked, sounding wracked with worry and guilt.

"It is very bad," the doctor said.

Mother's skin fell pale as she nodded. "Will she …" she began, faltering. "Is she going to …"

"She'll be fine," the doctor said with a half-hearted smile. "She just needs to stay here for a while so we can monitor her progress."

Mother thanked the doctor profusely and then tumbled into her chair the moment he left. The two of us were alone in this way for a while. Mom seemed short of breath, and no matter what I tried, I couldn't seem to beat back the tears that came to my eyes. The medicine the doctor had given me was helping with my clarity. I was no longer a raving lunatic child. But the pain had returned and redoubled. It was all I could do to keep from screaming.

I lay back on my pillow, my teeth clenched as I stared up at the heavily plastered ceiling. It was a typical room: square and white-walled and shabby. There was a sink, but no bathroom. The bathroom could be found just down the hall. There were two of them on the floor: one men's and one women's.

After a time, a new doctor entered the room, along with an entourage of nurses. One of the nurses—short, dark-haired, bespectacled—cleaned and prepared my wound. The doctor watched all this like any good supervisor. Then, when the wound was clean, he sat at the foot of my bed and began poking and prodding at my cut with apparent disregard for my suffering. He kept asking whether this hurt or that hurt, and of course every response from me was either *yes* or a wailing cry that must have been abundantly self-evident.

When the doctor finished, I tried to ignore my pain by watching the busy work of the nurses. It seemed that they were mixing plaster in a large bowl. Meanwhile, the nurse stepped in to wrap my wound in a fresh bandage.

"Just relax and lay back," she said. "We're going to set you with a cast."

I did my best to relax, but it was difficult with all this pain and activity. Mom held my hand tight. Whenever the pain erupted in my knee, I would squeeze her fingers until they turned white.

In time, the nurses had fit me with a cast, and the doctor had injected me with medicine that made me woozy. I must have fallen asleep, because when I woke, I found myself in another room, this one less private. I was on the end, near a wall dotted with a pair of windows, and there were three other beds to my right, each lumpy with another patient. Mother was gone, and I suspected it was because visiting hours had ended.

I craned my neck to look down at myself. My cast, it seemed, ran from my thigh all the way down to my ankle. I could still move my foot, but not without considerable pain in my knee. There would be little movement out of me until I began to get better.

For a week, I lay in this way, still quite sick.

By the second week, I began to feel better. In time, I felt so much better that I was able to get up and walk around under my own power. The doctors said that my cast could come off soon, and my mother and sisters visited me often. The visits were always welcome, but it meant that I would have to walk down the stairs to meet them. Visitors were not allowed in my ward, so I would have to go to the visitors instead of the visitors coming to me. Because the building was rather barebones, there was no elevator. That meant walking down the stairs—and for a girl in a full-leg cast, that was no easy task. I would hobble down with one hand on the support rail and one arm slung over a crutch. I eventually got better at walking down the stairs, but walking back up remained a problem.

Every two days, Mom or one of my sisters would visit me. On one such occasion, I was hobbling down the stairs when a tall young man with light brown hair came up to me and asked if I needed some help. I noted his light skin and green eyes and supposed he was part Russian.

"Are you sure?" he said when I shook my head.

Shyly, I told him no.

He passed me by, and even as he ascended the stairs, I could feel his gaze warm upon my neck. I did my best to move quickly, to get out of his sight, but it was difficult.

The next morning, after my physical therapy, I was walking down the hallway when the same young man came hobbling in the opposite direction. It took me a while to realize that he was imitating me, dragging his right leg as if it were stiff within a cast. I furrowed my brow, feeling my cheeks burn red. He grinned and continued limping. I scowled at him as he passed and then made my way into my room.

The room seemed smaller every time I entered. Shared by four people, it was difficult even stretching out in bed, let alone getting comfortable. And without a television, it was even more difficult to prevent oneself from becoming overwhelmed with boredom. Always the busybody, I would get bored quickly.

Later that same day, I decided to fight my boredom by heading back out into the hallway and trying to walk. Not five minutes into my laps back and forth in the hall, the young man came out again and started mocking me. Again, I shot him a dirty look and darted back into my room.

Several days later, I found myself alone in my room—certainly a rarity during my long stay. I was lying in my bed, staring up at the ceiling, when I noticed out of the corner of my eye the door swinging open. I turned to see who had entered, and was shocked to find that it was the boy who had been mocking me. I frowned at him scornfully.

He came directly to my bed, stood and looked at me for a while, and then handed me a piece of paper.

"Here," he said.

And before I could respond, he bolted from the room.

Confused, I opened the little wad of paper. Inside, I found a few lines of wobbly handwriting.

"Please be my girlfriend," it said. "Say yes!"

My face grew hot in an instant. I had been embarrassed many times in my life, but never more than I felt in that moment. Given that I was alone in the room, my embarrassment was perhaps a little silly, but I felt it all the same. Immediately, I buried the paper under my pillow, the only place I knew to hide something like this. I then plopped my head down upon it, fuming and mincing about what had just transpired.

This was the first time I had ever received a note from a boy. I didn't know what to think. So, under this deep confusion, I would roll over every couple of minutes to retrieve the paper and read it again. Then I would bury it back under my pillow. One moment, I would find flattery; the next, fury. I couldn't decide whether this strange young man was actually interested in me or was just making fun of me.

It wouldn't be until the next morning, after my therapy, that I would get a chance to meet him face-to-face again. The moment I saw him turn around the corner and into the hallway, I dropped my chin to my chest, not wanting to make eye contact. Still, I could feel his approach, and could sense that he was making his way directly toward me.

"Hi," he said to the top of my head.

I looked up with a frown.

"My name is Chuka," he said. "Do you have an answer for me?"

The heat returned to my cheeks. For a moment, I simply stared at him. Then, without a sound, I pushed past and walked away.

For the next few days, we would meet in this same way, and he would always say the same thing: "My name is Chuka. Do you have an answer for me?" And I would always push past without a word. By the fourth day, I had had enough. I had spent all night thinking about our next encounter and what I would say to him, and I finally had worked up the nerve to speak.

"Why are you making fun of me?" I hissed when he posed the question again.

"What do you mean?" he asked, pressing his fingers to his chest and looking about as innocent as a young man in love can look.

"With the limping," I said. "You hurt my feelings."

His eyes widened. "I'm so sorry! I was just trying to get your attention because you weren't looking at me at all."

I scoffed and turned my head away. He bounded back into my field of vision, trying to hold my eyes.

"I just did that so you would say something to me," he said. "I didn't care what. Just *something*."

We stared at each other for a time, Chuka hopeful and I frustrated.

"So do you have an answer for me?"

With another scoff, I pushed past and went straight into my room, slamming the door behind me.

That evening, my doctor entered my room with a small group of young people trailing him. They came immediately to my cot, everyone staring down at me with hopeful and blinking eyes. I retreated into my defensive posture, feeling and looking like the shyest girl in all Mongolia. I listened as the doctor explained that he was lecturing to students this evening, and then tried to grasp all that I could of what he said to the students about my condition. Little did I know that this would be more than just a one-time introduction. From that day forward, my doctor's four students—three young women and one young man—would be my primary caregivers. Each day, they would arrive around the same time to examine and treat my leg.

At first, they huddled over me like any doctor would over any patient. But after a few days, I began to notice that the male trainee would stick around longer than the others. He would always linger at my bedside to ask one last question. Then, one last question became one more inspection. And then one more inspection became the occasional small talk.

He introduced himself as Bayraa and would be no stranger to me and my leg in the days that would follow. I didn't mind the attention because Bayraa was remarkably handsome. Still, I didn't think anything of it until one day when he asked me if I would be his girlfriend.

"Excuse me?" I asked, shocked.

"I was wondering if you would like to be my girlfriend," he repeated, clearly trying and failing to sound clinical and professional.

"Um," I said, and that was all I could manage. Red-faced, I pulled my blanket up to my chest and turned away. I could feel Bayraa lingering behind me for a time, but after a few long seconds, he shuffled away.

That night, I could hardly sleep. I couldn't believe what was happening.

Never in my life had a boy my age ever shown even a modicum of interest in me, and now two boys were asking me out at the same time.

For the following few days, I would receive two visitors to my room: first Chuka and then Bayraa, each of them bringing expensive candies to offer. Whenever they arrived with a new treat, they would pose their question again, and I would continue to waffle.

It was a difficult decision. But in the end, it was a sense of humor that won the day. Both men were tall and handsome, but it was Chuka who made me laugh. So by the end of my third week in the hospital, I was telling Chuka that I would be his girlfriend and then breaking the bad news to Bayraa.

Bayraa was upset and didn't mind showing it. He refused to accept my decision, an act that would represent only the first in a long measure of resistance to the first man whose heart I broke.

CHAPTER 12

There was something about that spring. It was one of the most beautiful single seasons that I could ever recall, and with it came my recovery.

Eventually, the doctors removed my cast, and I was able to walk around less impeded than before. It would be a while yet before I could walk with a normal gait, and longer still before I could get back to my contortion training, but it still felt good to be without a cast and able to walk the grounds of the hospital without major strain.

One afternoon, I decided to take a stroll outside to the small park behind the hospital. The moment I sat down on the wrought-iron park bench closest to the hospital grounds, Chuka came up behind me and placed his hands on my shoulders. I startled, then giggled when I realized who it was.

"You shouldn't scare me like that," I said to him.

Beaming, he sat down beside me. We made small talk for a time as we watched the tall grass wave and the sun trace lower against the horizon. He told me about his family and about what had happened to him to ensure such a long stay in the hospital. For the first time, I felt like the two of us were getting to know each other. It was peaceful and it was serene, but the moment would not last.

"Hey!" I heard from behind.

I turned to look in the direction of the yelling, and saw the unmistakably lanky outline of Bayraa heading in our direction. I tensed. Chuka placed his hand on my leg as if staking claim to his prize.

"What are you doing out here?" Bayraa demanded the moment he reached us. "Hey!" He pointed down at Chuka's hand, which remained on my leg. "Get your hands off my girlfriend!"

I drew a breath to protest, but before I could speak, Chuka spoke for me.

"She's not your girlfriend," he said. "She's mine."

Without warning, Chuka leapt over the bench and began tussling with Bayraa. The trainee grabbed the patient by the collar, and the patient grappled with the trainee's waist. I stood and whined at them to stop. They didn't listen. Bayraa reared back and cracked Chuka on the jaw. Chuka was fazed only for a moment before returning the punch with one of his own, connecting squarely with Bayraa's ribs.

"Stop it!" I hollered. "Please, stop!"

The men traded a few dull thwacks against each other's cheeks before toppling to the earth in a mess of limbs and fingers. I kept yelling, now for help.

In short order, every door behind the hospital opened and out poured a small army of nurses. With grand efficiency, the nurses descended on the two fighters and pulled them apart. Several of the nurses began hollering for the meaning of this. Chuka and Bayraa just panted and glared at one another. And there I was with my hands clasped behind my back, terrified that I had somehow gotten us all into grave trouble.

I said nothing, and the nurses took this as a sign that what they had seen was what they had believed: two young men, one of them a doctor in training at this very hospital, were fighting over the affections of a patient. It was all they needed to haul the boys away to one room and me to my bed.

To my great surprise, the following day brought quiet. I had expected some kind of repercussion, but none came. Later than usual, Chuka arrived to bring me chocolate. He smiled as I gingerly touched the swelling over his right eye. I asked him what happened with the nurses, but he only shrugged and said that they were sorting things out.

Later that day, I heard from the other trainees that Bayraa had been transferred to a different hospital. I felt sorry for him, but glad that he didn't get fired altogether. And then I felt wretched about my role in all this. I wondered whether there was something I could have done differently to avoid such an unsettling feud.

Apart from my mother and sisters, my partner would come to visit me often in the hospital. As it happened, she would visit me on one occasion the same day I had my first kiss with Chuka. I could barely speak after the kiss, and spent the rest of the day either glowing or preening. She was quick to notice.

"Are you hiding something from me?" she asked.

"No," I said defensively.

"I know you," she said, furrowing her prominent brow. "You're definitely hiding something from me. What is it?"

I kept silent, only able to manage a smile.

She began to nod. "You have a boyfriend, don't you?"

My jaw dropped. I could hardly believe I was being that transparent. "How did you know?"

She offered one of her trademark mischievous smiles. "I want to meet him."

Through a grin, I sighed. "Wait here." I went to fetch Chuka.

My boyfriend was happy to accompany me outside to meet with my training partner. He always seemed to have more questions for me regarding my profession, and I suppose he jumped at the chance to get a third-party opinion on the matter.

I don't remember what the three of us talked about for the few minutes that Chuka remained, but I do remember being a sublime combination of nervous and proud. My boyfriend was funny and handsome, and he had Uugii grinning, laughing, and shaking her head in subtle awe.

After a time, Chuka went back to his room, leaving her and me alone to gossip.

"He's so tall and good looking" she said.

"You sound rather surprised," I said, and she smiled.

"How did you meet him?"

I explained all the drama with Chuka and Bayraa to my wide-eyed partner. She had many more questions for me following that little revelation, and I did my best to slake her curiosity.

After nearly four weeks in the hospital, I was finally discharged. I was happy to be able to go home, of course, but sad that I would have to leave Chuka behind. I got right back into contortionist training—so my life got busy in a hurry—but I made sure to always make time to visit Chuka in the hospital at the end of the day. For some reason, my partner would always ask if it would be all right for her to join me on my visits. It felt strange, but I couldn't say no because she was essentially my cover. If my mother or coach ever found out I was dating, they would lose their minds. It wouldn't be a good thing for me if they discovered my secret.

I took my little secret-keeper with me to the hospital for several weeks after.

Finally, Chuka received his own discharge. This would have been a sad day for the both of us, if not for his aunt and uncle taking him in. His parents lived in another town, after all, and if he had had to go home to stay with them, he and I would have seen each other only rarely. But his aunt and uncle lived in my town, so we would be allowed to meet as often as we had grown accustomed to meeting.

It would be a short-lived romance, as first loves often are. The time came when Chuka had to return to his parents and, as he told me, go to school in the city. He promised to write me every day, and for a while, he kept that promise. He would also call me from time to time, as his father worked in a government office and was fortunate enough to have access to a telephone.

—⟪⟫—

Four months after Chuka's departure, the latest countryside tour was announced. My rehab and training had gone well, but not well enough that I could yet travel with a group with any kind of consistency. It was a bittersweet thing to learn that the contortionist set to go in my stead was Uugii. My sadness at missing my opportunity to see Chuka again was only equaled by my hope that my partner could do her best to pass on my love to him.

"Let him know how much I miss him," I said to her.

She promised that she would.

The tour was set for forty-five days, and I counted all forty-five because I longed to learn from my partner how my boyfriend fared.

Chuka continued to call and write, of course, but I wanted to learn from someone else that my love was okay. Whenever he would call, I would withhold the knowledge that my circus was sending a troupe to his hometown. I wanted it to be a surprise, after all. And as the tour date came closer, I had a tougher time keeping my secret inside. I don't know whether he noticed that I was holding something back, but he did seem to grow more distant the closer the date became.

Finally, the day arrived when I knew that my partner would be visiting Chuka and sending my love. I waited patiently for a letter or call, but none came. Days passed. Then weeks. And still no word from my boyfriend.

At first, I figured Chuka was simply too busy to call or write. With school and work and his home life, he would often run himself ragged.

After the longest forty-five days in my life, the tour finally returned. I couldn't wait to ask my partner about my boyfriend. I waited in our dressing room for her, anxiously hoping to catch her before she left the building. Of course, in my excitement, I forgot that it was customary for performers to take a few days off following a long and arduous countryside tour. So I was disappointed to learn that she wasn't even in town.

These were the most difficult days, these last few in waiting for her. I had worked up in my mind that Chuka had given her a tremendous love letter to pass on to me, and that the letter itself was the reason he had decided not to call or write since the day the tour had stopped in his town. I couldn't imagine what might be contained in this letter, but I was sure of its existence and its potential to make me overwhelmingly happy. I imagined his elegant turns of phrase, his professions of love and lust, his dire hope that we could reunite in the near future.

Three days later, the traveling group returned to work. I waited in my shared dressing room for my partner to bring the letter to me. I saw her before she saw me. She passed by my door, walking past as if it were like any other in the building—nothing special, no one important housed therein. I leapt from my chair and took off after her. When I caught up to her, I tapped her shoulder.

She turned. Where I expected the childlike joy she often showed upon seeing me, I found nothing but indifference.

"Oh, hi, Otgo," she said blandly.

"Well?" I said expectantly.

She shrugged. "Listen, I'm not feeling well. I got sick on the way over here and need to go home. Can we talk tomorrow?"

Confused and a little frustrated, I nevertheless agreed. "Okay, girl. You feel better, okay?"

Nodding, she left me there in the bustling hallway, feeling violently alone with my thoughts. I stood there for a time, pondering what all this might mean. I tried to remain levelheaded about it, but in the end, my girlish curiosity got the better of me. I ran to the dressing room of another performer I had known for a long while. Her name was Altai, and she was older than my current partner and me, but I figured if anyone in the troupe could be trusted to be discreet about my inquiring of a boyfriend, it would be her.

"When you guys were in Khentii Aimag," I asked delicately, "did you see a tall young man with blonde hair who answered to the name of Chuka?"

"Oh yes," Altai said. "Of course I did!"

"Was he ... good?"

Altai suddenly donned a strange expression. "He was good. Yes, good."

The two of us stood staring at one another until it felt too awkward to continue. Something sat funny with me, and I walked away feeling strange.

The next day, I sat alone in my dressing room, wondering if I might finally get my opportunity to speak with my partner. So when I heard a knock on my door, I perked up.

"Come in!" I called.

It was Altai, and not her, who entered my room. Sweat formed on my brow.

"Otgo," she said timidly, "I wanted to talk to you about something because you and I have worked together so many times, and I've known you for such a long time."

Good news is never preceded by such words. I could scarcely breathe.

"I'm sorry," Altai said. "I just can't be quiet about it anymore because it's too hard for me to look at you every day and still hold onto this secret."

My heart began to race as I stared at her.

Altai's face contorted in a strained sort of way. "At first, we were told that this Chuka was your boyfriend."

I swooned at the very mention of his name.

"But not too long after he first arrived, your boyfriend became pretty close with another performer here."

"Pretty close? What do you mean?"

"*Very* close."

"Very close? What do you mean?"

Altai sighed. Instead of answering my question, she continued her story with head hung low. "Chuka came every day to visit her after our shows. Most of the time, they didn't stay in her room. They would go back to his house. They did this the whole time we were in town."

I felt as if I were pinned to the chair. Tears began to form and then flow over my cheeks.

"I'm so sorry to be the one to have to tell you all this," Altai said. "But you just had to know."

By now, I was crying so hard that I didn't care to sit in front of Altai anymore. I bolted from my dressing room and into the shower, where I sobbed openly. Something inside my chest felt heavy. I wanted to tear it from me, but it was trapped within, accompanied by the feeling that it could never be removed—a lead weight I would have to carry for the rest of my life.

I couldn't stop crying. It was difficult to believe what I had heard and yet not difficult. For the first time in my young life, I knew what it meant to have your heart broken.

On the fourth day following the return of the traveling circus, my partner finally showed her face at work. I had been waiting for her, scanning the crowd of incoming performers to find her. I saw her weaving between a few performers, looking like she was either in a hurry or trying not to be seen. I waited for her to reach the dressing rooms before I pounced.

"I know what happened," I said even before she could turn around to see who was darkening her doorway.

She turned slowly, and with one raised eyebrow, said, "What are you talking about?"

I knew in my heart in that moment that I would have to be the one to stop this. She didn't tell me about what happened with Chuka and this other performer. But what could I do? It was too late.

I shrunk away from my former friend, unable to follow through with my anger.

A couple of months after my confrontation with my partner, I received a phone call. As fate would have it, it was Altai who would enter my dressing room to inform me of the call. Confused, I went down the hall and to the lone phone that we all shared. With no idea who might be calling me, I pressed the phone to my ear.

"Hello?"

"Guess who," came the familiar voice.

I groaned inwardly.

"It's Chuka!" he said.

I kept my silence, feeling my fingers run numb.

"Otgo? How are you?"

I hung up the phone without speaking, and I went up to my dressing room. He called again. Again, someone came to fetch me. This time I asked the messenger to tell the caller that I wasn't here. I just couldn't stomach the thought of speaking with him.

After that day, Chuka called a few more times. He also wrote me a letter. But I would always ask whoever answered the phone to tell him that they couldn't find me or that I wasn't around. I never read the letter. I simply wanted nothing to do with him anymore.

Seven months later, I had just changed following a particularly grueling practice when I exited through the back door of the circus building. There, I ran into none other than Chuka, who had been waiting for me. The moment I saw him, my heart skipped, but I didn't say anything. I simply walked on past.

He jogged a few steps to catch up with me. "Hey, Otgo!"

"I don't have anything to say to you," I said. I walked faster, trying to lose him.

"What? What do you mean?"

He kept jogging along after me, pleading for me to speak to him the whole way to the bus station.

I paid for a ticket and got on the bus. Chuka did the same. All the while, he kept talking to me, trying to get me to say something. He tried to be charming, tried to be angry, tried to be pleading. None of it worked. We rode the whole way to my bus stop in this way, Chuka flapping his gums and I remaining silent with my arms crossed defiantly over my chest.

When the gate opened at the front of the bus, I rushed to get out. Chuka, clearly startled, followed. As soon as I got to the gate, I turned and barred his departure.

"I don't have anything to say to you," I said.

"But, Otgo—"

"And I don't want to have anything to do with you," I spat. "So goodbye!"

With that, I made my way down the walk toward my ger. The last I saw of Chuka, he was standing by the gate, looking bewildered and a little sad.

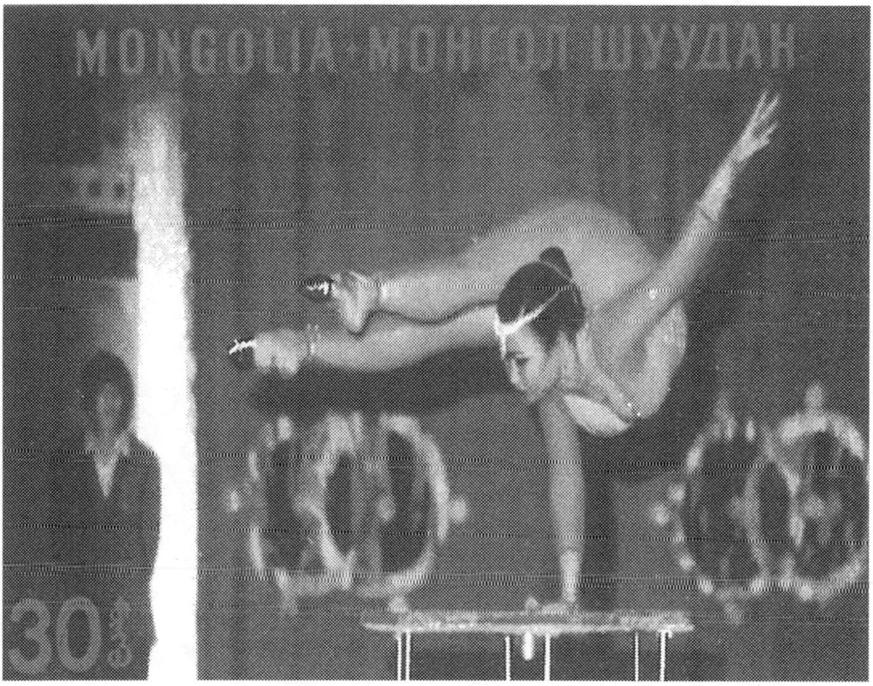
MONGOLIA · МОНГОЛ ШУУДАН
30

CHAPTER 13

⁓ ⁂ ⁓

In 1986, I would experience the most important and most intimidating concert tour of my life. This was Mongolian Cultural Day, and it would take us to such exotic places as Moscow, St. Petersburg, Minsk, Poland, and England. A large group of dancers, singers, and other performers from the Mongolian Folk Dance Ensemble would be mandated to perform, as would many ballerinas, singers, composers, and actresses from the opera. And then, of course, there were four contortionists, including me.

As excited as I was to visit a few places I had never been before, I was most excited about a place I had been to many times: Moscow. I have always felt drawn to Moscow. Even to this day, I think about it often and remember it as my favorite city in the world. Perhaps it is its unparalleled architectural beauty. Perhaps it is its colorful people. Or maybe it's just because I once saw a movie called *The White Night Melodious* that has always resonated with me. Such a lovely movie. In it, a Russian man falls in love with a Japanese woman, and St. Petersburg plays a substantial role.

Of course my favorite place in Moscow is Red Square, which in 1986 was perhaps at the peak of its glory. The military precision of the square is awe-inspiring. And the grand panoramas of old buildings, with their ornate awnings and rooftops, always left me short of breath.

Despite what most might think, even under Communist rule, the people of Moscow were quite kind. Life was hard for them, but everyone seemed to bear things admirably. Of course, until I moved to a place where life was not so difficult, the fact that life was difficult in Moscow never really occurred to me. It was the same in Mongolia, after all. In any case, I could always get directions if I asked for them. And I could walk the streets alone without being bothered.

So the portion of the tour that took us to Moscow was obviously quite enjoyable for me. I visited the Red Square and the street of Arbat. I marveled at the shops and the brisk people. I watched several old Russian ladies plodding through the market. Such tough grace, such brutal pride these women had. It made me envious.

From Moscow, the tour would take me on a series of firsts. St. Petersburg was enlightening. What a beautiful city. In Minsk, we took a tour of the city in which I learned the story of Khatin, a story that has remained with me all these years.

When the tour guide began telling the story, our bus full of performers fell palpably silent.

"It was March 22, 1943," the tour guide said, his thick mustache dancing over his upper lip. "The Nazi army, having laid siege to the town for some time, entered the square and began burning everything in sight—houses, buildings, trees. Men, women, and children were burned alive inside their own homes."

As tough as my life had been, I couldn't imagine such a thing.

"Out of the whole town, only two children escaped the fires. They had been hiding in the woods, and so were spared the flames."

As the guide told us this wretched story, we drove through the restored town. All the doors were white, and each bore a single silver bell. They did this in remembrance of the dead.

After Minsk, our performance group was split into two. The first group, which included me and Uugii, would go to Poland while the second would visit England. I found Poland to be nice as well, with more of the colorful people I had so grown to admire outside my country.

———&———

During the winter following our tour abroad, I was on another of my favorite Mongolian countryside tours when a tooth on the left bottom side of my jaw became infected. The pain was almost unbearable. Almost before I knew what was happening, the whole left side of my face had swelled up.

At first, I fought the infection by taking aspirin, licking a stinky salt called *Omkhii Davs*, and otherwise just bearing it out. The treatment worked at first, but after two days, there was nothing I could do to dull the pain.

On the heels of the pain came tremendous sickness. I could hardly walk, let alone perform. A couple of days later, a performer friend of mine told me about a gynecologist who occasionally came in from a nearby town to check on pregnant women and any sick people who might need the aid of a doctor. This was a third-world country, after all, and a doctor, regardless of specialty, was expected to tend to all needs presented him.

In any case, as luck would have it, the gynecologist was available to see me. So my performer friend went to speak with the doctor, bringing him back to tend to me.

I felt sicker than I can ever remember feeling. Given my disturbing history with older men, I might have felt uncomfortable being alone with the doctor, but I was in so much pain and feeling so sick that trepidation about old men just didn't register.

The gynecologist looked at my tooth and said it had become infected.

"There's only one treatment at this advanced stage," he said. And then he scrunched up his nose. "We'll have to pull it out."

I looked him straight in his sad, gray eyes and told him that I didn't care what he had to do. "Just make the pain go away!" I said. I had to speak in looser terms because it hurt to either close or open my jaw all the way.

"I'm sure you know this already," the doctor said, fingering his bulbous nose, "but this is going to be very painful."

"I don't care."

"I don't have any Novocain."

"Just pull it out!"

The doctor rocked back in his chair, cupping his hand over his chin. "I have an idea." He nodded profoundly. "It might help with the pain of the procedure."

"What is it?" I winced, having spoken too aggressively for my jaw to handle. "I'll try anything."

"It's simple, really," the doctor said, holding out both hands. "You drink vodka. I pull your tooth out."

"No Novocain," I said.

He shook his head.

"Just vodka?"

He nodded and then shrugged. "Do you trust me?"

"Fine," I said. "I'll drink the vodka. Just do it quickly!"

The doctor then left the room to find vodka. After what felt like an hour of searing pain, he returned empty handed. "They don't have the vodka," he said. "I'll go out and get some."

I tried to sleep while he was gone, but couldn't. It felt like I had a heartbeat in my tooth itself.

Finally, the doctor returned with a standard bottle of vodka. He popped the cap, took a quick swig, and then handed the bottle gingerly to me. "Okay." He held his finger about a quarter of the way down from the neck of the bottle. "You drink this much. Then I'll pull your tooth, and you'll drink this much." He dropped his hand down to the halfway point of the bottle.

"Doc," I said, "that's half the bottle."

He shrugged.

With a slow sigh, I took a deep breath and a deeper sip. My tongue protested, and my throat burned. I gagged and nearly threw up. I looked at the doctor with pleading eyes.

"Well, don't breathe," he said. "I'll pinch your nose while you drink. That will help."

I drank as much as I could before gagging. I gagged several times as I took down the awful liquid.

"Don't throw up," the doctor said. "Just keep breathing as I pinch your nose."

Despite how horrible it made me feel, I did exactly as the doctor asked me. The next thing I knew, my stomach began to feel warm, and I got extremely dizzy. His face now a blurry mass, the doctor stooped over me and laid me down.

"Okay, now," he said. "I want you to lay flat. Wrap your arms around your stomach and hold your hands tight to your sides."

Despite my sudden drunkenness, I did as I was told.

The doctor picked up his left leg and used it to pin my arms to my stomach. I couldn't move. Visions of Sanaa came to my mind, and suddenly I felt with every ounce of my being that I needed to leave the room. Still, no matter what I tried, I couldn't move. I was drunk. I was pinned down. And I was alone. The terror was only outweighed by the pain in my jaw.

"Okay," he said. "Now I want you to open your mouth as wide as you can."

I did as I was asked, warm tears forming in my eyes.

"No matter what I do, you must remain still," the doctor said. "If you jerk your head, you're going to make it worse. So just hold still, okay?"

I nodded, pinching my eyes closed, tears escaping down the sides of my face and pooling in my ears. I kept my mouth as wide as I could as the doctor fetched a pair of needle-nose pliers. The pain I felt when he touched the cold steel to my infected tooth was blinding and white. I could hear a crackling noise as he moved my tooth a few times. Then, with a great roaring crack, he pulled the tooth from my skull.

Warm, thick liquid filled my mouth. I tried to scream, but couldn't because the pain was too great. I moaned and cried and tasted warm blood. The doctor crammed large swaths of gauze into my mouth, trying to staunch the flow of blood. He kept the pressure hard on my gums. This was a new kind of pain, but a much more tolerable one than I had grown used to experiencing over the previous few days.

A couple of minutes passed with the gauze before the doctor told me to rinse my mouth and drink the other quarter of vodka as he had instructed.

Woozy and overwhelmed, I shook my head in protest.

"Drink!" the doctor ordered. "If you don't drink as I tell you to drink, you're going to get sick."

Again, I shook my head.

"It will help you to numb the pain. Believe me; you don't want this pain for the rest of the night. The vodka will deaden it."

Finally, drunk, my head throbbing, I did as I was told.

When I finished my half-bottle of vodka, as prescribed, I fell into a level of drunk that I had never experienced before or since. I hadn't eaten anything in a week, and now here my body was expected to deal with so much booze and blood. I passed out fully and dreamily, and when I woke, it was all anyone could do to hear my story about the gynecologist without clapping their hands to their mouths and contorting their faces in pained disbelief.

So that was medical care with the traveling circus.

CHAPTER 14

In January of 1989, I was told that later in the year I would be traveling to Germany with three other performers. The trip would last four to five months, far longer than I had ever been away from home for one stretch.

When I told my mother about the trip, the first thing she said was that it was a long time. "I'm not sure I'll still be alive when you get back."

"Oh, Mom," I said, shaking my head at her melodrama.

Still, she had never said anything like this before, so as much as I wanted to pass it off as black comedy, something about it weighed heavily on my heart.

"I don't have to go if you don't want me to," I said.

"No, no," Mother insisted. "This is your job and your future. You have to go."

Feeling a little bleak about everything, I decided to leave with my troupe. There would be four of us: myself and two aerialists named Gerlee and Tsomoo, and then our boss, Namnan. We left in the spring—April, as I recall. We were to take the train from Ulaanbaatar to Moscow and from Moscow to Berlin.

At the train station, Mother began to cry. This struck me as strange, as I had traveled many times before, and Mother had never reacted this way. She had grown so accustomed to it, in fact, that she rarely showed any emotion anymore. She would simply wish me good luck and tell me to do the best job I could. "Never let your country or your family's name down," she would say.

But now she cried.

Seeing her this way caused me to cry too. "Mom, please know that it's a long time, but that I will be back as soon as we finish the tour."

She nodded, sobbing.

"You have to promise me you'll take care of yourself," I said.

Again, she nodded.

My heart began to race. "Mom, you would tell me if something was bothering you, wouldn't you?" And as I looked her over, for the first time I noticed that she looked rather frail. I had always known my mother to be an old woman—she was quite advanced in age when she had me, after all. But only just now had I seen its effects in her eyes. She looked weathered. Broken down.

"No, I'm fine," she said. "I'm just worried because you never leave for this long. Don't you worry, child."

My tears flowed freely now. How could I not worry after all I had heard and seen?

"You just remember what I told you before," she said. "Work hard. Never let your country or your family's name down."

The train began to move behind me. It churned slowly at first and then began to pick up the pace. I tore away from Mother and boarded the train. I found my cabin immediately and stuck my head out the window to wave goodbye one last time. Outside, I saw my mother crying as she ran, waving and following the train.

"*Menee oxen* (my daughter)!" she yelled. "Please take care of yourself always!"

The train began to move faster and faster, and soon my mother drifted out of sight. I was left with the troubling sensation that my mother had recently resigned herself to death.

For five days, we traveled by train into Moscow, so I was left with the sadness and nothing to do to assuage it. It was the longest five days of travel I have ever experienced. All the while, I carried the picture in my mind of my mother running after the train.

Finally, we made it into Moscow and then moved on to Berlin. In Berlin, we knew there was a family with the last name of Probst who had a private trailer to offer us. But we didn't know much beyond that. Our first show would begin the very second we stepped off the train, as the circus was already underway by the time we disembarked. Given that we didn't speak the language, we had no idea where we were to go to dress, how we would get to where we would be staying, how we would get our mail, make a call, or anything else essential to the traveling artist. Still, we made it to our first show, and everything went off without a hitch.

After the show, we managed to track down a member of the Probst family, and fortunately, he spoke Russian. Through him, we gathered the address where we would be staying and how we could contact our loved ones. I quickly penned a letter to Mother and sent it away.

For nearly a month, I waited for her reply, but nothing came. I sent another, fearing that the first had been lost in the mail, but no reply was returned. I wanted desperately to make a phone call, but my ger simply didn't have access to a phone line. In such darkness, I began to worry. The other three members of the traveling group had heard back from their respective families, but I had heard nothing. It was stranger still because I knew that Mother was always so prompt in her responses.

I kept thinking about that day at the train.

Weeks passed. With every day, I grew more concerned. I longed to go home.

Then one day I learned that the aerialist who was traveling with us, Lady Gerlee, had opted out of her contract due to pregnancy. There was a German woman who would replace her while she was on leave. So, knowing that Gerlee would be going back to Ulaanbaatar, I asked her if she would take a letter to my mother and deliver it personally. She was happy to fulfill my request.

So here I was now alone with two adult men. It felt strange and awkward. I thought often of Sanaa, but those thoughts were quickly allayed whenever one of the men appeared uncomfortable around me. Clearly, this discomfort went both ways. When I realized that fact, I calmed down a little. But my calm was only relative. I was still so worried about my mother, after all. My two companions were making phone calls to their family every couple of weeks, and I was left in the dark about what had happened with my mother and sisters. Why had nobody returned my letters?

The Probst family was a great comfort to me. The man of the house was named Ron. He was old, but kindly. His wife, Kristini, was a heavyset woman with rosy cheeks and motherly eyes. They had two daughters and a son, but the daughters were married with children and living on their own. Their son, Robert, meanwhile, was young, single, and incredibly sexy. Even before we got comfortable in the trailer, I could tell that Robert liked me, but I didn't speak German, so the mutual attraction sort of fizzled.

In response, I began to learn to speak German. This came from talking with the local performers and townspeople. One such performer was a tiger trainer named Klaus and his wife, Susanna. Susanna had just given birth to the couple's second child, a boy, just like the first. Another couple I grew close to was Peter and Mandy. Peter, a retired performer, was in charge of the maintenance to the circus tent while his wife was an usher. Through my friendship with these four people, the language came quickly for me. It was good to get to know the local culture, but mostly I appreciated the lessons because they helped me take my mind off my mother.

As if mirroring the tumult in my mind, one of the most stirring political events of my life occurred a month before the end of that long, difficult tour in Germany. It was late afternoon, and I was in my dressing room. Outside, people were talking loudly and running around.

Confused, I went outside to see what was going on. All the performers and the circus staff seemed to emerge at the same time. Many appeared quite excited.

"What's happening?" I asked of an older couple who was milling about beside the door.

"The two countries are becoming one," the husband said with a tearful grin.

"But what about the Wall?"

"They're talking about tearing it down!" he shouted over the din.

My heart leapt, and for the first time in what felt like years, I knew joy. I stayed and chatted with the couple about what the fall of the Berlin Wall would mean to our two countries. Then I retired to my room. Not long after I lay down, I heard a tap at my window. Then another. I rose up to see that someone was throwing pebbles at my window. I went to the sill and pulled the glass back.

"What?" I hollered down.

I could see that a few of my German friends were frolicking around on the street below.

"Come with us to the Western side!" one of them yelled.

As much as I wanted to be joyful and celebratory on the most important day of any of our lives, I could not help but feel burdened by the lead weight in my heart. My troubles were just too much in those days.

"I'm sorry," I said. "I can't come."

They protested, but I shooed them away.

The next day, my troupe, along with the circus itself, was light by a sizeable number of performers and staff. We would later discover that many people had left, fled the country to the greener pastures of the West.

CHAPTER 15

About a month before we were to finish our long German tour, Boss Namnan's wife and daughter came to visit. They bore with them a letter from my Norovsambuu. It was a surprise, this letter, and a foreboding one.

Feeling anxious, I tore open the envelope as I scampered back to my room.

"Otgo," it read, "I know it's very hard to hear, but your Mom is not doing so well. She is very sick."

Tears came to my eyes so thickly that I could hardly read on. Now I knew why I wasn't getting any letters from my family. Mother didn't want to trouble me while I was away. I cried quietly in my room, not wanting to share this further torment with anyone else. Anyway, no one had cared when I was having a hard time contacting my mother. Why would they care now?

After the initial shock wore off, I realized that Norovsambuu must be overreacting. Why would my brothers and sisters not contact me if my mother was terribly sick, after all? The only reason they would leave me in the dark is if mother wasn't that bad off. I had my doubts, but this seemed reasonable. I clung to this small sliver of hope for the final few weeks of the tour.

I went through the motions on all my performances like a woman who wanted to be anywhere else in the world but where I was. And it was true. I just wanted to finish. More than anything else, not knowing about what was going on with my mother was driving me crazy. I passed my free time with shopping for gifts for my family. I found myself buying far more things for Mother than I did for anyone else.

All the while, I would think about how I had left her, about how she had run after the train at the station, crying and calling out to me.

Mother was fond of many different kinds of fabric because she would use them to make traditional clothing for my brothers and sisters and me. Given her favor for traditional outfits, she preferred rich colors. So I bought her reams of deep reds and purples, so much that I could hardly carry it all. I knew that she would love it.

Finally, the longest wait of my life was over. It was time to return home. We departed Germany and passed into Russia. From Russia, it was a long flight to Ulaanbaatar. The moment we landed in Ulaanbaatar, my heart began to race.

I got in line at the customs service, trying to crane my neck to see around the crowd, trying desperately to find some sign that my mother had come. When I reached the head of the line, my eyes panned more quickly over the crowd. Mother wasn't there. It was at this moment that I knew my coach was right. Mother had to be terribly sick. Otherwise, why would she miss out on her ritual of picking me up at the airport?

Maybe she's waiting for me at home, I thought.

After a few more moments of looking, I saw my brother, Bayraa, and my sisters, Naraa and Enkhee. All three looked downtrodden, though they tried to smile when they saw me. When I came up to them, we all hugged and kissed and bid our hellos.

"Where is Mom?" I asked, tears already forming. "How is she?"

"Let's just go home first," Bayraa said, sounding exhausted.

"Okay," I said, shaking over the ominous feeling this gave me.

On the way home, I couldn't contain it anymore.

"How is Mom?" I asked of Naraa. "Is she really in bad shape?"

"Yes," Naraa said sadly, but that was all I could get out of her.

None of my siblings seemed to want to talk about Mother.

Finally we made it home. I bolted from the car, running inside the ger and calling for Mother. In short order, I found that she was not there. She wasn't in her bed. She wasn't in the yard. Nothing was right.

Then, just as my siblings entered the front door, I found something that made my heart stop. Just over the nightstand, I saw a big framed picture of Mother. This was Mongolian tradition upon the death of a loved one. I could scarcely breathe as I realized what the picture meant. The tears that came blinded me. I fell to my knees. I sobbed and fell onto the floor.

"I'm so sorry," Bayraa said. "Mom went to heaven, Otgo."

"No!" I hollered, going out of my mind with anguish. "Where is she?"

"I'm sorry," he repeated. "She's just not here with us anymore."

"*Eejee!*" I screamed. "*Eejee! Menee khairtai eej minee!*"

I don't remember what happened after that. When I woke, lying next to me were Bayraa, Naraa, and Enkhee.

"You should drink something," Enkhee said.

I reached out, and she handed me a mug of Tsai tea. The taste of it brought to mind memories of Mother, and I began crying again.

"Why?" I asked of them. "How?"

It was Naraa who would finally provide the answers I sought. "Mom died about a month and a half after you left."

"But why didn't you—"

"We will tell you more later," Enkhee interrupted. "But for now, we are worried about your own health, Otgo. You need time to settle down before we tell you any more."

After a couple of days, my sisters went home, leaving Bayraa and me alone in the house we once shared with our departed mother. It was difficult to live in this way, because Bayraa and I had once lived alone with Mother, and now it was just the two of us. I couldn't eat or sleep. I did little beyond crying. Many days passed in this same way—so many that

I lost count. I didn't want to go outside or do anything. I just didn't have any interest in anything but mourning my mother.

One night, I asked Bayraa what really happened.

"I want to know everything," I said. "Don't spare me the details."

With a profound sigh, Bayraa finally obliged. "Two months before you left, Mom started having blood in her stool. She didn't want to tell anyone because you were going to leave for work for such a long time, and she didn't want to worry you. She knew if you worried about her health, you might try to skip the trip. And then, of course, Mom didn't want you to lose your job."

I opened my mouth to protest, but Bayraa cut me off with a silencing wave.

"So anyway," he continued, "after you left, she finally went to see a doctor. The doctor found that Mom had colon cancer, and that it was already too late. She was given only a month to live."

"Why didn't you write to me?" I pleaded.

Bayraa frowned. "The doctor told us we should. He said if we didn't bring you back, you wouldn't be able to see Mom again while she was alive."

"But why didn't you—"

"Otgo, we did," he interrupted. "Noyo and Tsogoo went to the circus to talk to the producer. What was his name?"

"Mandakh?" I said.

He nodded. "That's right. Mandakh. Mandakh told them that if we brought you back from your tour, you would never work for his circus again."

Tears came to my eyes. I hung my head, furious and helpless all at once.

"Noyo and Tsogoo were shocked to hear that, of course," Bayraa continued. "So they left. They just didn't know what to do at that moment. They returned later that day to tell the rest of us. They talked about the whole situation with Mom, and we all decided to send you an emergency fax."

My heart sank. I hadn't been told about any fax.

"When we didn't get a reply, we sent the fax again and again. Nothing. So at that point, we decided that we shouldn't bring you back because it was already too late. Mom would die before we could ever get you home. And you would lose your job for nothing."

"It wouldn't have been for nothing!" I protested.

Again, Bayraa held up a silencing hand. There was a strange calm in his eyes, a level of maturity I had never seen in him before.

"Mom was getting sicker," he said. "So the doctors decided to open her up. They said surgery might help her hold on longer. That way, she could see you. None of us really held out any hope that she would recover. We just wanted to prolong her life to the point where the two of you could say goodbye."

It was all I could do to breathe, let alone stop crying when I heard these words.

"When they opened her up, they found that it was far too late. They left her open for a few days, coming back every now and then to clean her up inside. Mom kept asking about you." Now I detected a tear in Bayraa's eye as well. "She just kept asking, 'Is she here yet?' Whenever someone came into the room, she would lift her head and ask if you were coming. She just wanted to see you one more time before she died, Otgo."

I sobbed, falling into my brother's arms.

"Her last day," Bayraa said, sounding strained, "she just kept staring at the door. She passed away like that."

I pawed at Bayraa's back, feeling guilty and angry and terribly sad all at once.

"Mom kept fighting it," Bayraa said. "She held on many days longer than the doctors said she would, just trying to be alive so she could see you."

We both cried for a time, silently. Our bodies rocked and shuddered. We sniffled and sobbed.

"After she passed away," Bayraa said after a time, "we were all still hoping you could make it to the funeral. So we kept sending the fax. But we received nothing in reply. Noyo went back to the circus to tell your producer that Mom was dead, and he said he would spread the word, but no one came. We didn't even receive a condolence."

At that, all my sadness melted into rage. I was determined then to confront the man who had robbed me of my chance to see Mother in her time of need.

—◈—

My mother was dead. She had died not long after I left on my most recent tour, and she was buried before I returned home. Not until several months after her death did I discover what had happened. And I owed all this to my uncaring producer.

With all this roiling in my mind, I stormed through the back door of the circus building. A security guard sat at a desk beside the door, but he paid me no mind as I rushed to Mandakh's office. When I saw Mandakh's pleasant face, I nearly fainted. But I kept hold of myself because I wanted him to see how much damage he had done to me. I gritted my teeth, balled my hands into fists, and cleared my throat to alert him to my presence.

"Oh, my daughter," Mandakh said with a smile. "Come in, come in!"

It took me a moment to gather myself, and when I did, I began much more civilly than I had planned. "Bagshen-Teacher," I said softly, "I need to talk to you."

"What is it, daughter?"

To hear him call me his daughter made my blood boil. If I had felt any power over the situation, I would have spit in his face. I tried to calm myself, tried to remember what Bayraa had told me before I left that morning for my first day back at work.

"Don't let them be sorry for you," he had said. "If you are going to hurt them, they can't see your sadness."

"You didn't tell me about my mother," I said as calmly as possible.

Mandakh sighed, his round shoulders slumping as he shook his head. "I'm sorry about your mom. But we tried to contact you. And then we had no idea she would die so soon. I mean, I only just found out about her funeral today."

I fumed, wanting to hurt this lying bureaucrat.

"But you know," Mandakh said with a thoughtful nod, "one way or another, we all lose our parents one day. So if you need some more time off, go ahead and take it."

I drew a hot breath to yell at him, but then again remembered what Bayraa had said. So without a word, I turned and stormed from the room.

In the hall, I bumped into my coach. Seeing Norovsambuu's eyes for the first time in months reminded me of my mother. She seemed to recognize my pain, as her expression softened. She knew what had happened, of course. Our families had been close at one time. But she didn't appear to know what to say. Tears welling up, I bolted, not wanting to see her now.

I made my way to my dressing room, where I slumped down on the sofa and cried.

Not long after, I heard my door open. Norovsambuu had entered. She came immediately to my side and tried to calm me down. She rubbed my back and cooed that everything would be all right.

When I finally calmed down, the two of us sat, and for a long while, talked about my mother and all that had happened.

"You know," she said after a time, "the Director of the Women's Group has been asking to see you ever since your tour ended."

I sniffled. "I don't think I could possibly face her right now."

This was the woman who had spearheaded the movement to make me a supporting artist when I was caught smoking, so I figured that no good could possibly come of the meeting.

"You have to, Otgo," my coach insisted.

With a grand groan, I did as my coach instructed. At the end of the hall, I found the Women's Group leader's room. I knocked on the frame of her door, her door being open.

"Otgo," she said in a pleasant tone that sounded rather phony. "Come in!"

I stepped inside, my hands clasped behind my back and my eyes directed at the floor.

"I was sorry to hear about your mom," the woman said. "I didn't know at the time it happened or I would have alerted you."

I grumbled a halfhearted thank you, but she paid it no mind.

"Anyway, here is some money for your family."

When I looked up, I could see that she was holding an envelope out to me. I supposed that it contained a small wad of cash.

"I don't want any money," I spat.

"Just take it," she said. "This is how we help people in your situation."

I made a move to resist, but in a flash, she had stood and come to me. She grabbed my hand and slapped the money into it. As she glared down at me threateningly, I knew that I had no choice but to take what she had given. Communism might have fallen, but many of the old power structures still existed in Mongolia and elsewhere. I couldn't cross this woman or it would be the end of me as a performer.

When I returned home, I told Bayraa about what had happened. He was angry that I had taken the money, viewing it as charity we didn't need.

"You should have just left it there," he said. And as I cried apologetically, he counted the money, which turned out to be less than T200. To be given charity was one thing. To be given such small charity—that was an insult.

After all that I had endured on that day, I felt like quitting. Between my boss playing the martyr and my Women's Group leader shoving small bills into my hand, I didn't know if I could take it anymore. I paced and ranted around the room, unable to get hold of myself.

"These people are like animals!" I screamed. "I'm never going back there again!"

Bayraa watched me for a time, looking either confused or worried. To me, it didn't matter which. I was too angry to care about anything or anyone but my departed mother.

We carried on like this for several days—Bayraa taking silent stock of my situation while I paced around like a mental patient, vowing never to return to work. In time, even Bayraa couldn't stay any longer. He went back to traveling the countryside in his job as an electrician.

It was lonely for me after Bayraa left. I filled the void by drinking.

This was something that was new to me, this heavy drinking, so it hit me hard at first. But I continued on, day after day, because the alcohol helped me forget about Mother.

I began to develop into a raging drunk. When my sisters came to visit, no matter how much sympathy they showed me, no matter how much they wanted to help, I would holler at them to go away.

"I don't need you," I would yell. "I don't need anybody!"

Things were not the same without Mother around. My home became colder and darker. Nobody ever visited. The refrigerator was always empty. When I was sad, I would drink. When I was tired, I would drink. When I was hungry, I would drink. I took up smoking to calm my nerves. Nothing helped.

Before long I had lost a great deal of weight. In my depression, my entire world turned upside down. Everything was dark, black, dead. I would stay up all hours, lamenting my mother, my best friend who I was never able to say goodbye to.

"She's gone," I would whisper to myself through long pulls of vodka. "How could this happen?"

I found myself missing everything about her. Her smell. Brushing her hair. Talking to her about nothing. I missed how she used to get upset with me. I missed the light in her eyes whenever she met me at the bus station. I missed the way she used to linger over me with that maternal look of urgency etched across her face.

"I miss my mommy!" I would cry. "My mommy was everything to me!"

I was nineteen years old, and I was crying for my mommy.

I felt robbed. Robbed by my family's inability to contact me. Robbed by the circus and its producers. Robbed by the bureaucratic machine of my government. Robbed by Communism.

I dreamed about my mother almost every night. Some dreams were nice. Others were nightmares. Later, they became recurring. In the dreams, everyone in my life knew about my mother's health except for me. I imagined them keeping it from me like some kind of grand conspiracy, some kind of cruel joke.

On one of my darker days, my friend, Namraa, had come to visit me.

"Have you been to visit your mother's grave?" she asked.

"Of course not," I said. According to Mongolian tradition, if your parents die, you don't visit the grave for three years following the funeral. As much as I wanted to break this directive, given our special case, my family told me not to go.

"That's ridiculous," Namraa said. "It's a stupid tradition. If you want to go, I can find a car so we can go together."

Feeling a glimmer of excitement for the first time in weeks, I readily agreed.

"Where is she buried?" Namraa asked.

I frowned. I didn't know. I tried to describe the place as best I could based on what I had learned from Bayraa.

In time, Namraa began to nod. "I think I know where that is." The next day, we piled into a car and drove off. For an hour, we searched and couldn't find anything. But then, just as I was about to give up hope, we found a lonely hillside graveyard.

I bolted from the car in search of Mother's grave. When I found it, I tumbled down upon it, hugging her gravestone and screaming, crying, and apologizing into the air.

"I'm so sorry!" I yelled. "I'm sorry for not being there, and I'm sorry I didn't even know you were gone."

I sat there for a long time, just crying and talking to her. There was nothing else I could do.

In time, Namraa came up to me and placed her hands on my shoulders. "We better go now. We've been here a long time. It's getting dark."

I said goodbye to my mother, and we left.

CHAPTER 16

It was early December of 1989. Now that my mourning period had ended, Norovsambuu asked me to come back to the circus because she had signed a contract for a duo act to work in Romania for two months. So I did as my coach asked.

At the time, Romania was one of the poorest countries in the world. When we arrived, I found it to be cold. It seemed almost everything was frozen in ice. Everyone seemed to be on food stamps. When we went to the grocery store, we found it almost empty. The people seemed worn, depressed, sad. I immediately began to wonder how we would ever make it to the New Year in a dark place like this.

The one beautiful thing I found in Romania was the circus building. It was quite impressive. There was a hotel connected to the building, so that was where we all stayed. This made it easier for us because nobody wanted to go outside.

Two weeks passed. One night, before the show, we were all getting ready to perform. Everyone was warming up, and show time was fast upon us, but no one had arrived. We had no audience. Our audience director and the sound and lighting crew were missing as well.

"What's going on?" someone shouted.

A few minutes later, one of the local managers came to us and said there would be no show today.

"Why the hell not?" someone asked.

"Riots," the manager said simply.

And we were all left there wondering how in the world a man could be so calm about a riot—as if it were commonplace.

"What kind of riot?" someone called after him.

He shrugged, his little frame rising slightly. "Not sure. All we know is that you need to stay in your rooms. Just watch TV. Don't go anywhere."

"What about tomorrow?"

"We'll let you know."

We went back to our rooms, confused.

The next day, we went back to getting dressed for what we hoped would be our first show in two days. But the manager came to us and said the riots were getting bigger and that the circus had decided to cancel the shows for the entire week.

"But don't go outside," he warned. "It's too dangerous."

We all went back to our rooms again, thinking this was a strange and hard place, this Romania.

By the third day, we began to hear gunfire. We began to lose it, running around the halls of the hotel, trying to figure out what was going on. Everyone was shouting for the local circus manager, but he was nowhere to be found.

In time, we were visited by a police officer, who calmed us down and told us that the circus director couldn't make it, but that he told him to pass along some information. Apparently, the riots had become a civil war, with the civilians fighting the government's army.

Some of us began to panic.

"Don't worry," the officer said, and his thick mustache danced over his lips. "We have soldiers protecting us here. They have the building surrounded. Please just do not go outside or look out your windows, and you will be fine."

An explosion erupted outside. A few of the women screamed.

"The TVs will work, but the phone lines have been cut," the officer continued. "And try to make whatever food you have last as long as you can."

"We're under siege?" one of the men shouted.

"It looks that way," the officer said.

More panic erupted.

"Just please be patient."

I looked into the huddle of nervous stage performers and saw that my coach was frightened. This was the first time I had ever witnessed fear in her eyes. I knew right then that we would die here. I went to Norovsambuu and took her into my arms.

"I hope your mom and dad are watching over us," she said.

"I know they are," I said.

"Yes. We will not worry."

But it was clear to me that my coach was worried.

We both returned to our room, trying to get some sleep, though it was the middle of the day and we could still hear the war raging. We tried watching TV, but it was no use. And there was no good to be had from eating food.

The next day, we lost power, and our rooms got colder and colder. Gunfire began to erupt nearby. And it was this that triggered the brave among us to demand that we go to our embassy.

"We'll be safer there," Norovsambuu insisted.

As my coach assembled a traveling party, I tried to use the bathroom. But I couldn't. I had been going more often than was usual of late, and now I couldn't go at all. I tried to force myself, but it was painful. And in the end, blood was all I could produce.

A high fever followed. Outside, the gunfire continued, and inside we had no medicine to treat me. The pain was tremendous.

In time, it was decided that I would go to the hospital before moving on to the embassy. I felt terrible being the reason that the plans were changed, but Norovsambuu insisted.

I don't remember much about the ride, as my head swirled with the pain I was under. When we arrived at the small hospital, I awoke to a place of carnage and chaos. I grew woozy at the sight of all the wounded people.

A grizzled doctor looked me over for half a minute before telling Norovsambuu that I had a urinary tract infection and probably a kidney infection too. He gave me a shot and a bottle of pills before offering a bed for the night. But Norovsambuu decided to take me to the embassy because she felt it wasn't safe there in the hospital.

Norovsambuu called the embassy, who told her that it wasn't safe to walk the streets outside their building.

"But we need medical attention!" Norovsambuu shouted.

I winced, bending half-wise in my little cot.

She mumbled something about a plane. "They were going to send a plane," she told me then as she sat down beside me, "but they had to shut down the airport."

I asked her why, but she didn't know.

A call came in several minutes later. Rebels had tried to bomb the plane in flight, so we were stuck.

"What about the train station?" Norovsambuu demanded.

They had taken the train station and the airport. The situation was getting dire. We had to just sit and wait, the cacophony of rioting and bombing our only soundtrack.

A couple days later, I was feeling a little better. Our troupe's elephant trainer knocked on our door to tell us that we had to watch the TV.

"They're going to execute Ceaușescu and his wife!" he hollered.

This was the leader of the party in power.

We turned on the TV and huddled around. I watched as they brought the proud but broken political leader into the middle of the square. He was a slight-chinned man with a hooked nose and a broad forehead. Beside him was his wife, who quivered, but stood tall. She was plain, but still pretty. Her hair was dark and her features decidedly and romantically Romanian.

And then without warning, the rebels opened fire. Both of them went down at the same time.

We all screamed at once. I felt my skin crawl. To see two people executed right in front of your eyes … it's not something you soon forget.

After the execution, it got even crazier outside. After a time, our guard got a call in on his radio informing us that we couldn't drink the water because the rebels had poisoned it.

The circus building was shot at several times in the night. Gunfire became a constant. A bomb exploded right outside our hotel, kicking up dust in the muddy streets.

The embassy finally contacted our guard, informing us that they were on the way to pick us up. We were already ready. When they arrived, it was in a series of armored cars. They told us all not to look outside, to keep our heads down. They filed us to the front door of the hotel. My stomach burned. I felt okay lying down, but now running hurt me badly.

At the door, we were greeted by a huddle of soldiers with machine guns. They hollered some directives, and then pushed through the door. I squinted in the gray light of morning. And there I saw what was happening firsthand for the first time. Men were firing at each other. There were bodies in the street. Fires burned here and there. A tank had been stationed just down the street. There was far less shouting and crying than I ever would have guessed. It was all so silent between the gunshots.

The ride to the train station brought more horrible sights. More bodies, more tanks, more explosions. It was like watching a war movie, only I had a part in this one.

When we arrived at the train station, we were met by a person from the embassy. This man had successfully negotiated with the rebels about sending us on the train back to Russia. The train was to take diplomats and their families, but they made room for us because Norovsambuu was famous and I was sick.

"Be very careful," the embassy negotiator said. He had the darkest and yet most comforting eyes. "Close the curtain in your car. Lock the door. And be aware of everything. If you make it safely through to Russia, you will be okay."

On the train platform, it was chaos. We had to pass through several security checkpoints before we finally arrived at our train. The embassy negotiator kept flashing his diplomatic passport, and that was our ticket to board. Thank God for him, and for the embassy soldiers too.

It seemed that everywhere we turned, they were patting us down for weapons. But finally, we made it to our compartment on the train and closed and locked the door. We opened the window to the platform, shouting our thanks to the embassy negotiator, who waved and told us to keep our window closed.

Norovsambuu and I toppled down into our seats, praying. The train began to move. I lay down on the bed, my fever having returned. The train made no stops in Romania, plowing on into Russia. It was the quietest train ride of my life. I suppose that's because everyone was too frightened to speak to each other.

By the evening, we had reached the Russian border. A great cry of joy rang out.

The checkpoint at the border was understandably tight. They had soldiers and dogs to search us, but no problems were uncovered. Because my coach had many connections, we were able to secure a room at the Mongolian Embassy's guesthouse. As soon as we arrived, Norovsambuu's doctor friend checked me out and gave me a shot, some medicine, and the first plate of hot food I had seen in days.

The next morning, I woke up very late, feeling much better already. We explored the embassy. Everyone who worked there was Mongolian, so it was nice to be around our own people. There was even a Mongolian restaurant on the sixth floor. We ate some banshtai tsai and buuz. It was the greatest feeling to be healthy and safe.

"It feels like I'm home," I said to Norovsambuu.

"I know," she said with a sad little smile. "I feel the same way."

Later that day, she went to the airline to book two flights back to Mongolia. Our flights wouldn't leave for two days, so we had some time to kill. We went to see the New Circus of Moscow, which was a nice treat following our difficult ordeal in Romania. We had been in a war zone two days earlier. And now here we sat, watching high art in Moscow. We were lucky to be alive.

It was a couple of days before the New Year when we returned to Mongolia. After a long flight home, I was greeted by my brothers and sisters, who were all relieved that we made it out of the country. They had been watching the riots and then the revolution on TV and didn't believe we would make it. I headed home and switched on the TV myself. There I saw that the fighting continued. Seeing the gunfire and death on television made it all seem so distant. The fact that I had only just left this place of destruction and chaos was just so surreal.

With all that had happened—The fall of the Berlin Wall, the death of my mother, and now surviving a terrible illness and a revolution in Romania—I found myself not caring about work again. Norovsambuu began telling my friends to ask me when I was coming back to work. I would always tell them to pass on the notion that I was sick. I didn't go to work for a long time. At that point, I was so tangled up inside that I didn't even care if they fired me. Surprisingly, I didn't get into any trouble over my long absence. Not even Mandakh gave me a hard time.

I shut myself down completely. I ate little, slept little. I rarely left the house. My sisters began to express worry. They tried to talk me into going back to work and getting my life started again, but I didn't listen to anybody. Oyunaa was there for me often. As was Grandpa Sharav.

It would be the latter who would finally spark me out of my long bout with self-pity. I was over at Grandpa's house, eating his famous Khuushuur, when he said to me, "I know it's been very difficult for you to deal with your mother's death, but I think your mom would be happy if you went back to work."

My shoulders slumped as I realized it was true.

Grandpa continued on with a generous smile. "I remember she loved telling everybody that you were traveling and what present you would be bringing her."

I remembered then that Mom used to love talking about me with her friends and neighbors. I knew that Grandpa was right. At the same time, I felt sad to think that I couldn't make her happy again. Warm tears came to my eyes. I tried to stop them, but I couldn't.

I noticed then that Grandpa had tears in his eyes too. "My child, you're the one who has to take care of your parents' name. And with you carrying on the tradition, they will rest in peace."

My Grandpa Sharav. I am so grateful for him, even to this day.

When I finally did return to work, I found myself tagging along with a different company, this one a Folk Dance Ensemble called Mandukhai. The producer of the company was named Dolgor.

"We're going to travel overseas very soon," she told me. "So be here tomorrow for rehearsal."

The next day, I did as I was asked. I found it wonderful to get back to work. Ms. Dolgor introduced me to the other performers, who seemed like nice people. And no one was all that hard on me about whether and how I should practice. Ms. Dolgor said she liked my act. She even offered me a place to stay in her home.

"Just so you don't have to be alone," she said.

"Thank you for the offer," I said with the best smile I could manage. "But I'm used to being alone by now."

"Aren't you scared?"

For a moment, I wanted to cry again, but I held back. It was nice to have somebody caring about my feelings, especially considering that she didn't know me at all.

CHAPTER 17

It was early 1990 when word spread that I was still living alone. One night I was watching TV when someone knocked on my door. I was frightened, not wanting to greet someone I didn't know in the middle of the night. Whoever it was continued to knock for a while, but then eventually stopped. Relieved, I assumed that the caller had left.

I got up from my seat, and at that moment, I heard a crash at the gate. Shortly thereafter, I heard a wrenching at the door. My heart raced. I considered running, but felt frozen to the floor. When the door crashed open, the first thing I noticed was that I recognized the men. They were two men I worked with—other performers. I noticed that they were inebriated.

"You're a contortionist," one of them said.

I nodded.

"You get to travel overseas."

Again, I nodded.

"Then what's wrong with you?"

I raised an eyebrow, confused.

"What are you still doing in this country?"

And with that, they left.

—◦◦◦—

Since the incident with my intruders, I felt a strong urge to move elsewhere. I knew that I would be safer living alone in a nicer neighborhood. So I started asking around as to whether anybody knew of a room for rent.

A lady I worked with at the Mandukhai Ensemble told me of a lady friend of hers who was a musician. The musician needed a tenant.

"She lives by herself," my coworker said. "She has a daughter, but the daughter lives with her grandparents."

This should have sent up warning bells in my mind—the fact that this woman's own daughter didn't want to live with her—but at the time, I was so desperate to get out of my ger that I was oblivious.

"The room is small," my coworker said, "but it should work for you."

"I don't care if she has me sleeping in the living room," I said. "I just need to go somewhere where nobody knows me."

Later that day, I met up with my coworker's friend, a woman named Solongo. She showed me the room for rent, a tiny space equipped with a glass door. Though the door was glass, at least I knew I would have some privacy. I paid my rent for a few months in advance, which Solongo liked very much.

So I moved from the ger of my birth to the west side of Ulaanbaatar. I told no one of the move—not even my family. In my mind, it was the best way to ensure that no one would bother me anymore. I knew that if I told my sisters, they would only worry. So I kept it to myself, making perhaps the first decision I ever made on my own in my life.

—◦◦◦—

Life began quietly in my new room. My landlady came home and introduced me to her friend, a skinny, short-haired woman named Tuya. We sat down and talked for a while, the three of us, and I didn't notice much odd about Tuya, except that she had a way of staring, her eyes lingering on me and staring through me as if looking well into the distance. I thought nothing of her, particularly since they made short work of our conversation, saying that they were headed to a party.

I enjoyed another night alone in safety.

A week later, Solongo invited me to Tuya's birthday party. Having spent the whole week at home, I found myself bored enough to agree to come along. Not long after leaving, I knew that I had made the right decision. Tuya's apartment showed that she lived the good life. She had furnishings far nicer than anything I had ever seen in person. The only thing strange about the party was that Solongo and I were the only guests. We sat down on a comfortable leather sofa. Tuya sat in the armchair across from us.

"My husband's out of town," Tuya said, her eyes staring through me again. "I'm just waiting on one other friend of mine. Then we can start the party."

Shortly, her friend did arrive, and the party indeed began. Tuya served us piles of home-cooked food and more expensive alcohol than I could ever want to drink. The other three women at the party were much older than me, so it was uncomfortable for me at first, but after a few drinks, I began to relax.

"Don't worry that we're older," Tuya said as if reading my mind. "We're all performers. So what? Just relax and have fun."

As the night progressed, I got more and more comfortable. We all talked and drank and danced. I was sweating from the dancing, so I went into the other room. Solongo joined me.

"So what's the story with Tuya?" I asked.

"Oh, she's married to a Czech guy," Solongo said. "They have a twenty-year-old daughter who's married."

"Why isn't her husband here for her birthday?"

"Oh, he's never home. She's pretty lonely, really."

Feeling sorry for Tuya, I went back to the party. The four of us had a nice time that night, drinking and dancing into the early hours of the morning before crashing out for sleep. The three guests would sleep on

Tuya's living room floor. Tuya herself would sleep in her own bedroom. I fell asleep early, exhausted and drunk as I was.

Not long after I fell asleep, I woke to the sensation of being touched on the breast. I thought I was dreaming, so I tried to fall back asleep. But then, the sensation returned and I woke up fully. In the darkness, I could see that someone was lying beside me, and whoever it was did indeed have a hand on my breast.

I leapt to my feet and ran to the wall, where I flipped on the light switch. Just as the lights came on, I saw Tuya disappear into her room. I was confused.

Not wanting to wake the other women, I switched the light off right away. Shaking it off, I went back to sleep.

Again, not long after I was out, I was woken by the sensation of being touched. When I came to fully, I tried to sit up, but I couldn't. Someone was lying on top of me, pinning me down. I could feel a hand sliding from my breast down to my leg, then moving between my legs.

I screamed. My attacker rolled off me. I heard a loud thump to my left. I jumped up to my feet and ran to turn on the lights. There, I saw Tuya on the living room floor, naked and flailing.

"What are you doing?" I screamed.

At that, the other two women woke up.

"What's going on?" Solongo asked, looking groggy.

I pointed an accusing finger at Tuya. "She was on top of me and touching me!"

"No, no, no," Tuya said. "I didn't do that. You were dreaming."

"Yes, you did!" I hollered.

"No, no, no."

"If you didn't do it, then what are you doing out here, naked and lying on the floor?"

Tuya took on the most dramatically offended look. "I got really thirsty. I was looking for something to drink and I thought I was in the kitchen. I must have stepped on you, Otgo. That's why you thought I was touching you."

Hot anger came to my face. I drew a breath to yell at her again, but Solongo cut me off.

"Let's just go back to bed," she said. "It doesn't matter. Just go back to your room, Tuya."

Tuya's friend told me to come lay next to her if I was having nightmares. Furiously, I waited for Tuya to return to her room. I switched off the light and went back to bed.

Lying now beside Tuya's friend, I had a woman on either side of me. I figured this would make me a little safer. Still, I couldn't get back to sleep. My anger and confusion were just too great.

Maybe she's just so drunk that she got confused, I thought. *She must miss her husband, after all.*

And at that thought, my anger was replaced by pity. Soon after, the sun came up and I left, thinking this would be the last time I would ever see Tuya.

The next day, I was at work when one of the performers came up to me.

"Otgo," she said, "there is a lady here looking for you. I think it's your sister."

I gave the other performer a funny look. My sister never came to visit me at work. So I came down from my dressing room, confused.

My confusion wouldn't last long. As I rounded the corner, I saw none other than Tuya. I glared at her as I approached. She took on an expression of either guilt or lust—it was difficult to tell with her thousand-yard stare.

"Can you come outside?" she asked.

As much as I wanted to yell at her, I didn't want to cause a scene, so I agreed to join her outside. The cold air enveloped us from the moment we stepped through the door. I could see my breath as we spoke.

"I'm so sorry about last night," Tuya said. "I was so drunk."

I glared at her for a while longer before my anger melted to acceptance. "Okay, fine. I understand you were a little drunk. Just don't mention this again, and we'll be fine. Let's just pretend it never happened."

"Of course!" Tuya said. "Yes, yes, that sounds great. Exactly what I was thinking."

∽

Two weeks later, I came home after work to find Solongo partying with a couple of her friends. Tuya was one of them. I tried to walk past unnoticed, bolting straight for my room. But they saw me.

"Otgo, come and party with us," Solongo said.

I knew that even if I said no, they wouldn't leave me alone all night, so I agreed. We had a couple of drinks, and then the other friend went home, leaving Solongo, Tuya, and me behind.

"I'm going to bed," I said. "I have to get up early for work."

"Okay," Solongo said.

"Good night," Tuya said, her voice laced with honey.

As I made my way toward my bedroom, I heard Tuya say she was too drunk to drive home.

"You can stay here for the night," Solongo said.

My heart dropped. I wished that I could lock my glass bedroom door, but there was no lock. I had asked Solongo if I could have one installed, but she told me no. Still, I got ready for bed and was soon asleep.

In the middle of the night, I heard the sound of my door cracking open. Then, before I realized what was happening, I heard footsteps on the floor. I pretended to be asleep until the footsteps shuffled near me. Then, I reached over to the nightstand and switched on the light.

"Tuya!" I barked. "Do you need something?"

Tuya leapt onto me. I tried to push her off, but she was too strong. She pinned my arms to the bed. I squealed. Visions of Sanaa returned to me. All the bad memories rushed into my mind. This man, hungry like an animal. And now Tuya had pinned me to the bed.

Furiously, I fought against her, but she did not give ground. I screamed and cried. She clawed at my arms. I got hold of her and finally pushed her to the floor.

Before she could collect herself, I ran from the room. Tuya gave chase.

I could hear her feet thumping the floor behind me, feel her breath hot on my neck. Just as she got her hands on me again, Solongo's door flung open and my roommate stepped into the living room.

"What's going on out here?" she said. "Are you guys fighting?"

"What fighting?" I said, crying wildly. "She's trying to touch me."

"*Touch* you?"

"It's not the first time!" I wailed. "You remember. Her birthday party."

"What are you talking about?" Tuya spat. "I didn't do anything. I went into your room because it's warmer. I was just trying to lie down in her bed, and she thinks I'm trying to touch her. She freaked out and started screaming and punching me."

Beside myself with shock, it took a moment for me to answer. But when I did finally answer, it came as a scream. "You *liar!*"

Solongo tossed her hands in the air, turning for her room. "I'm not going to take sides. You two are adults. You figure it out for yourselves."

I wanted to protest, but she held up a hand over her shoulder to silence us. "Just don't scream anymore. I'm trying to sleep." And with that, she closed the door behind her.

I ran back into my room and pulled my bed in front of the door so it wouldn't open. Tuya stood outside my door, tracing her hand over the glass.

"Otgo, please open the door."

"No!" I hollered. "Go away!"

She gave me the saddest, most pathetic look I have ever seen. "Please, Otgo. I just want to tell you something."

"No. I don't care what you have to say. We have nothing left to talk about."

"I'm sorry. I promise I'm not going to bother you ever again, but I have to tell you something."

Fiery anger came to my cheeks. "No! Don't you understand? No!"

My attacker stood outside the door, apologizing to me in many different ways, but I held my ground. Finally, I gave in.

"If you try to touch me again, I will punch you. Hard. I'm not kidding."

Tuya promised me she would not touch me again, so I opened the door. She came inside. I told her not to get close to me, and she agreed, standing back.

"Do you know why I'm doing this to you?" she asked.

"No, I don't. I think you are very sick."

Tuya's eyes began to water. "I'm in love with you."

I fell back onto the bed, in shock. I couldn't believe what I was hearing. "What? Why are you in love with me? You should be in love with your husband."

"I … I just …"

"You are a woman, and I'm a young girl. Men and women fall in love with each other, not two women of different ages. What kind of sickness is this?"

I was so naïve then. I had honestly never heard of a lesbian.

"Well, now you know," Tuya said sadly.

"You are married," I spat.

Tuya then took on a dreamy, far-off look. "When I was a student in the Czech Republic, there was a Czech lady who taught me everything. Being with a woman is magical, Otgo."

I wanted to throw up. "Never! I will never be like you, Tuya! You do whatever you want to do, but leave me out of it."

"You should try it," Tuya said softly. "You might like it. I can teach you."

"Try it with another person. I'm done."

Tuya then stood and tried to come near me, but I backed away. "Why don't you understand me? I have a heart."

"Well, I'm sorry," I said. "But I have my own heart too, and it loves men. Please leave."

With that, Tuya stormed out of the room, slamming my door so hard that the glass cracked. Now in the kitchen, she began screaming and whining like a crazy person. Solongo came out from her room and yelled for Tuya to stop the drama. In time, she took Tuya back into her bedroom, and it was quiet for the rest of the night.

I wish I could write that that was the last I would hear about the matter from Tuya, but obsession is a powerful thing. She would stalk me outside work. She would show up at parties that she wasn't invited to.

And everywhere I turned, it seemed that Tuya was waiting in her black car, staring at me. One time, I tried to confront her, and she threatened to kill me.

"You must be with me!" she screamed from her car. "If you won't be with me, I'll run you over."

She took off like a crazy person, swerving at the last minute to miss me.

After that, I always asked my male friends from the circus to walk me home. I had to change my apartment again. I lived with friends for a while, then secretly stayed overnight in my dressing room for a few weeks. This was very much against the rules, so I would have to dress in the dark and avoid the security guards at all cost. It was a stressful situation, but it was better than facing my stalker.

CHAPTER 18

In the winter of 1990, the director of our circus greeted us with big news. There would be an American talent agent coming to see the Mongolian State Circus. If we performed well in front of him, there was a chance he would hire us away to America. Everyone was giddy, as they all dreamed of moving to the land of the free. I was the lone exception.

Most of the performers prepared for the audition with extra care, but I would always try to make an excuse that would get me out of training. Norovsambuu would beg me to train so I could show my act, but I had no interest.

In Mongolia at the time, the visit of an American agent was big news. It threw the entire circus into disarray, everyone rearranging their performances and practice schedules to accommodate the audition. The auditions would be spread across three days, each performer getting an opportunity to perform on one of the three days. My coach spent much of the time leading up to the audition trying to jockey me into position for the first day, but I told her again and again that I didn't want to do it. "I won't win," I said. "Let me just go home."

I had never seen Norovsambuu angrier. "Just show your act, and your duo act too."

"But I haven't trained in weeks," I protested. "The Americans are going to pick the famous contortionists, not some girl who travels the countryside every year. I'm nobody."

"What's wrong with you? Other people are dying to show their act. You know your parents would have wanted you to do this."

I was defeated the moment Norovsambuu mentioned my parents. Of course she was right. I had no choice then but to perform.

Before my acts were set to begin, I sneaked around the curtain to take a peek at the panel who would be watching my performance. Sitting at a long table at the foot of the stage was the director of the circus, a couple of other Mongolian directors, and two older white men. One was bald and heavy and the other handsome with black hair and blue eyes.

When my name was called for my solo act, I felt more nervous than I ever could have anticipated. Still, I performed admirably and without mistake. When I finished, I had to run off stage to change for my duo act, which was set to begin next.

The duo act didn't go nearly as well. My partner and I failed to complete a few of the tricks. I left the stage early—even before the judges could say anything to me—because I knew that Norovsambuu would be angry.

The next day, due to embarrassment, I didn't return to work. The day after, I went back, sure that the Americans would have left by then. At least then they would have picked their choices and I could go about my days as I had before all the ruckus began.

But when I rounded the corner and headed toward the back door of the circus building, I saw a pair of white men exit a car and head in the same direction. Wanting to show my respect for the esteemed agents, I waited by the door and allowed them to go in ahead of me. As they passed, I noted that they all smelled very nice.

Without saying a word to me, they entered the building and went straight to the circus director's room. I asked around later and learned that they were still in Mongolia beyond schedule because they hadn't yet seen all the acts. So, instead of performing, my friends and I got to watch the remaining programs.

All the while, I kept looking at these Americans.

"The bald one is the one who makes the decisions," my friend told me. "The other guy is from an Italian agency. The lady is the sister of the bald guy."

I noticed the woman for the first time. She appeared to be middle-aged, smaller, and with black hair.

The next day, the director gathered all of us together for a meeting.

"The Americans will be back in three months," he said. "At that point, they will let us know which acts they have chosen."

Everyone groaned—everyone except me, anyway. Looking back, I think my reluctance to care about the Americans stemmed from the propaganda I had heard since I was a small child. Mongolian television, particularly under Communist control, was good at convincing Mongolians that Americans were racist bums who killed each other for fun. The whole thing reminded me of what I had experienced in Romania, and I had no desire to experience it again. If the Americans never came knocking on my door, that was just fine with me.

Later that year, in the early summer, the Americans sent a letter to let us know which acts were chosen. The first was Strong Man Amarjargal. The second was a set of drums acrobats. Twenty dancers had been chosen from the folk dance ensemble. And then the final acts chosen were one duo and two solo contortionist acts. The Americans would return in late summer to take pictures of the performers for the program book. Then, all the performers would be traveling to America in November.

Because the contortionists were not listed by name, the circus fell into chaos again. They had to decide on their own which contortionists were fit to go. All the directors, producers, and coaches got together for a meeting to determine which contortionists would be chosen.

I really didn't care about any of this because I knew for sure that I would not be the one to get picked, so I came to work whenever I wanted. If I didn't feel like it, I never showed up.

After they made their decisions about the contortionists, they held a meeting to announce who would be going. I wasn't at the meeting, so I had no idea who was chosen. My coach apparently looked all over for me, because when she couldn't find me, she called my sister, Naraa.

Naraa immediately called me at my new apartment.

"Otgo!" she screeched. "You're going to America!"

I sat in silent shock. I just couldn't believe I had made it.

Feeling like I was riding a cloud of confusion, I took the bus to the circus building and went immediately to talk to my coach.

"You guys made it!" Norovsambuu squealed as soon as she saw me. I had never seen so much pride in her eyes. "You and your partner are going to America!"

I could hardly breathe. Nothing like this had ever happened to me. I kept thinking about Romania, about how bad things always seemed to happen when I traveled to new and exotic countries. America. It just didn't seem real.

"We must start training every day," Norovsambuu said.

And so it was.

As fate would have it, Uugii would decide that she didn't want to go to America. She was married at that point and just didn't want to leave her husband behind. Her decision nearly made me back out of my agreement, but Norovsambuu lobbied for a new partner and convinced me to stay on. It seemed that my coach was determined to send me away. The belief was that I was alone, living in an unsafe home, suffering through attacks and verbal abuse, and as such, was due some good fortune. Norovsambuu believed that America was my good fortune—and she wouldn't have it any other way.

At the beginning of August, the Americans returned. They took many pictures and made many promises to take us away in the middle of November.

The closer it came to the established date, the more famous we all became in Mongolia. It seemed the whole country was talking about us. The circus directors, I guess having stars in their eyes, made sure to meet with us all before we left to make us swear to a two-year contract in America. After that, we were to return to Mongolia to perform as stars in our own country.

It was time. My siblings all seemed quite worried about me. They believed as I did that America just wasn't a safe place.

Two days before I left, my siblings and Grandpa Sharav got together in my parents' ger to have a going-away party for me.

Grandpa kept making me promise to return to Mongolia in two years. "Don't stay in America," he pleaded. "I don't think I'll be here much longer than that. And since you are like a daughter to me, I don't want to think that this is the last time I will ever see your pretty face."

It was difficult for me to say goodbye to Grandpa Sharav. I had already lost two parents, and to think about saying it again to a third was almost too much to bear.

Apart from these difficult goodbyes, we all took the time to sing, eat, and drink. It had been a long time since all of us were together in one house. Not since before Mom died did we all get together like this, in fact. It was nice to be around everyone at once.

"I don't want you guys to worry about me," I said to them. "I'm going to take care of myself, and I'm going to be wary while I'm working in America. If I can find more work, maybe I will be able to afford to bring you all over to visit me, as well."

It was Naraa who strode forward to speak for the group. "Just please take care of yourself. Don't worry about us."

We partied until late. Nobody slept much that night.

When we arrived at the airport early the next morning, it seemed that I was one of the last performers to show up. The terminal was full of people, everyone flashing pictures, crying, hugging, some of them leaving their wives, husbands, and little babies behind. Pretty much everyone was crying, save for the four contortionists, who were too young to have significant others to say goodbye to. My siblings and Grandpa Sharav might have made me cry, but we all believed that crying before a journey was bad luck.

"See," I said to Naraa. "There's no reason to worry. It's not like I'll be alone in America. I'm going with forty Mongolians."

Naraa, despite her obvious sadness, laughed in agreement.

When it was the time to go inside the gate, I kissed and hugged everybody. This is one of the toughest things I have ever had to do. Grandpa Sharav was the most difficult to say goodbye to, because I wasn't sure whether I would see him alive again. He was a very old man.

As I walked down to the gate, I looked back. Everybody had tears in their eyes, including Grandpa Sharav. The old man waved his hands to me with a smile on his face, but his eyes were lined with tears.

On the airplane, my seat was near the back. Looking out the window, I could see Bogd Uul. At that moment, I thought about how far I had come. I came from an improbably poor family. I grew up in a Socialist country. I had lost both my parents and had endured countless other emotional scars. Mongolians used to say, "*Deeshee khashgeraxad tenger xol dooshoo oroxod gazar khatuu!*" (When I scream up to the sky, it's too far away; and when I want to go down on the ground, it's too hard!) That was exactly how I felt as I sat on that plane. So I promised myself right then that it didn't matter what America brought me, I would stay there. I would start my life anew on a new continent. I would turn my life around, would avoid the mistakes of my past. And one day, when I was happy with my life, I would return to my native land.

I looked out at Bogd Uul, closed my eyes, and began to pray. "It doesn't matter how long it takes," I whispered. "I will have a better life. And when I have that, I will come back to my country."

With a roar, our plane took off down the runway and then departed the land.

When I looked out the window now, I could see the whole of Ulaanbaatar, everything getting smaller and smaller.

—◦◦◦—

After a stop for the night in China, and after nearly twelve hours of flying toward America—during which I was awed by the first big-screen television I had ever seen, flickering movies from the front of the plane—our translator got on the PA and announced that we should all change into our traditional Mongolian outfits because we would soon be landing in America.

Soon after, we landed. When we deplaned, the three people who had come to Mongolia for the auditions came forward to announce that they would be accompanying us on our flight from Los Angeles to another city I had never heard of.

"Welcome to America," the bald one said, and I was overwhelmed by the concept. Until that moment, traveling to America had seemed like a distant dream. And now here it was, real.

Following a long plane ride, we were to board a bus into a city called Tampa Bay. The flight seemed like the longest yet, given that it was our third long journey in as many days. I stepped off the plane exhausted, but startled by the incredible heat and humidity.

It's the middle of November, I remember thinking. *Is it still summer here?*

I spent the rest of the evening sweating and feeling like I was still on a plane. After our ride into Tampa, we all piled onto yet another bus and traveled to a nearby town called Venice, where they had a circus set up for our arrival. By the time we checked into our hotel, it was almost three straight days of nonstop travel.

We learned in the coming days that we would travel by train on a tour across much of America. The train would be private: a circus-only train. Unfortunately, it wasn't finished yet, so we would have to stay in our hotel for two weeks. We spent the first days around the Tampa area exploring the giant circus building. I read the sign above the stadium seating and realized for the first time the name of our company: Ringling Bros and Barnum and Bailey Three-Ring Circus.

Our guides in the building showed us everything. They introduced me and my partner to our contortion table, which was far bigger than anything we had ever worked with—so big, in fact, that someone would need to drive the table up to the stage.

Later that month, our hosts told us that they were going to take us to a big bird dinner, which was apparently an American holiday—but at the time, it meant nothing to us. We were just glad to have the feast.

In all the bustle of coming to America, I hadn't really properly met anyone. I also still didn't know the names of the men who had hired us. I would get my chance to learn them during my second week in America.

The bigger of the two of them approached the other contortionists and me one day while we were practicing. The bald gentleman said a few things to us in English, but none of us understood him. He smiled, gave us candy, and then went away. Later, through an interpreter, we would find out that the man had introduced himself as Tim Holst. The lady who helped him was Suzanna. And the handsome fellow who always seemed to be with them was Mr. Murillo.

Another week passed before we would finally be moved in to our permanent quarters: the train that the circus had constructed just for us. I had never lived on a train before, so it was a strange experience for me. There were three cars of varying sizes. The dancers were given the smallest car, with the acrobats and strong men occupying the second. The four contortionists, our boss lady, and the strong men were granted the biggest and nicest of the three cars. I couldn't believe my luck.

I would wind up sharing an otherwise private room with my new partner, Tseegii. Being that she was the youngest at fourteen years old, Tseegii made for a good roommate. We each had a double bed, and we shared a small refrigerator, closet, and table. I bought a hot plate and pots and pans to cook our food. In the middle of the train, there was a community shower and two bathrooms we all had to share.

I loved the freedom of almost living by myself, even if we all shared a shower and bathrooms. Despite having to share my room with my partner, I felt very much my own woman. I had never lived somewhere so new.

My paycheck turned out to be the only disappointment. I would be making $180 per week, which was fine, considering that I lived rent-free, but it was frustrating because $180 represented only 20 percent of what the American circus was paying us. The Mongolian government took the rest. Still, my only expenses were for food, drink, and the Laundromat.

At first, the American lifestyle shocked us all. It was like night to day when compared to where we came from. In the middle of December, Mr. Feld, one of the local guides, wanted us to join him for another holiday celebration called Christmas dinner. We had no idea what Christmas was, but we were again amazed by how much food was available to consume.

Getting together with Mr. and Mrs. Feld, the Feld daughters, and Mr. Tim Holst felt like meeting with a strange new family. Mr. Feld gave everybody a gift from the company. Atop the gift was a greeting card that read "Merry Christmas & Happy New Year."

Right next to where we had our train stationed was a highway, and over the highway was a big shopping center called Wal-Mart. I went over there one day with some of the other performers and was absolutely overwhelmed by what I found inside. I had never seen a store like that in my life. I wished I could buy everything I wanted—which was plenty—but I had very little money. I could only afford small groceries.

I went up to the register with my purchases and was blown away again by how Americans paid for their items. The man ahead of me in line rang up dozens of items before scanning a little plastic card through a big metallic block. The cashier gave him his receipt; he put his bags in his cart and left. I couldn't believe it. I had heard that nothing in America was free, but that certainly looked free to me.

After I paid for my groceries, I strolled toward the door, looking around for the people I had come with. I was the first to finish shopping, I guess, so I had to wait. As I waited, I watched a man walk up to a tall computerized box, holding another of the plastic cards I had seen at the register. He stuck his card in the box, pushed a few buttons, and then waited as the box spewed out money.

I stood in awe of the magic box. I wanted to tell my siblings about everything I had seen on that day, but the magic box was chief among them.

Finally, after a month of rehearsal, we were ready to perform our first show. The audience, as it turned out, was packed with people from all over the country because this was the first time in history that Mongolian performers had performed in America. Most of the Americans I spoke to had never heard of Mongolia before, but they were always intrigued by the exotic nature of our culture. We always had a full audience. Many times, people would come back to our show multiple times. It seemed they loved the colors, the culture, and the tradition of our acts.

I must say that the feeling was mutual. I loved that show and everything about it. It was the best I had ever been a part of.

CHAPTER 19

None of us spoke English, save for our translator, so whenever I would see a group of my fellow performers walking around, it would almost always be with translation dictionaries in their hands. At the time, I spoke a little German and Russian, so I was able to communicate with a German man I met who had worked for Ringling for many years. His name was Gerhard, and he was such a nice person, truly instrumental in my becoming acquainted with American culture.

Gerhard began to teach me English almost from the moment we met. At the same time, the Russian performers taught us how to make international calls. I would call my sisters, brothers, and Grandpa Sharav as often as I could afford it, always sharing with them all the interesting new things I was learning.

Following our run of success in Venice, our show traveled through Florida. One of our stops was at Disney World, which of course none of us had ever heard of prior to our arrival. We only knew that Mr. Tim told us it was one of the biggest parks in the world.

When we arrived at Disney World, my first impression was that I felt like a little kid for the first time in years. It was our day off, so we had all day to ride the rides. I rode everything, it seemed, playing nonstop.

The way the tour was structured, we would stay in a big city for a week, followed by smaller cities or towns for three to four days. Between each city, we would have a moving day, which was our day off. Whenever we moved, they would load everything onto the train, including the animals, equipment, and people's cars.

In this way, we traveled north across America. Three months later, in late March, we were in New York City performing at Madison Square Garden. To say that I was awed by New York and its many sights would be a vast understatement. I got to know it well over the two months that we were in the city—attending parties thrown by our company, meeting up with people like the Mongolian ambassador, and riding the subway all over the boroughs. Many performers invited their wives or husbands over from Mongolia for this leg of the journey, so it was a joyous time, those two months in New York.

The first year proved to be a long one. Many of the performers started dating each other. Others became lovers. Meanwhile, I was lonely and bored. I tried dating a man named Max, but that didn't work out so well.

By the time the second year began, I had learned a great deal of English, but I was well aware that I needed to learn more. I knew that it would help me meet people—and, more important, aid in my dream to remain in America beyond my current contract. I kept silent about my aspirations because everyone was told that they had to return to Mongolia after our American tour was over.

My silence would be broken by Mr. Tim Holst one day. I was between shows, walking down the corridor by the office trailer. The office door was open, and in it stood Mr. Tim.

"Hi, Mr. Tim!" I said to him.

Mr. Tim gave me a funny look. "Come up here, Akto."

I did a double-take, not used to Mr. Tim speaking to me directly.

"Come inside," he said again, waving his hand into the trailer. "Come, come."

A little frightened—this was my boss, after all—I did as he told me. When I got inside, he closed the door behind me.

"Sit," he said, pointing to an easy chair opposite his desk. "Sit, sit."

I sat.

"How is everything going?"

"Good, good," I said.

And then he took on a strange look. "I was wondering, Akto—" Mr. Tim couldn't properly pronounce my name for the longest time, "—are you planning on returning to Mongolia when your contract is up?"

"Yes!" I said, and I scolded myself for saying it too quickly.

He stared at me with a skeptical look, holding his concentration on me until I broke.

"No," I admitted. My heart was pumping so hard that I could scarcely breathe.

"What do you mean, no?" he asked.

"I don't want to return to Mongolia, Mr. Tim," I said in broken English. "I have nothing there."

His expression softened, melting to concern. "What about your mom and dad?"

"I don't have a mom and dad. They're both dead. I don't have a home."

Mr. Tim frowned and crossed his arms over his chest. He kept silent for a time, looking like he was thinking hard on something. My heart raced.

"You're not supposed to tell me these things," he said finally. "People don't usually tell me they're staying in America, anyway."

I just sat there quietly, feeling mortified. Still, I knew I had done the right thing. Mr. Tim was my boss, and you're not supposed to lie to your boss.

"Well," he said finally, "how do you plan to stay if you don't have a job?"

"I don't know … I don't have anything lined up. I just know that somehow I'm going to stay."

He shook his head and laughed, and I felt a great deal of the tension leave the room. "It's not so easy to survive here. Just promise me you'll think things through before you make your final decision."

"Okay," I said as cheerfully as I could manage. "Thank you for your advice, Mr. Tim."

As I rose and left the room, I couldn't believe what I had said to my boss. If he sent me home, I would be in big trouble with the directors at the circus, to say nothing of the politicians who might want to sanction me. My mind was spinning.

—⚬⚬—

The next day, after the opening of our latest show, Mr. Tim came up to me. "Do you have any video or pictures of your act?"

"No video," I said, struggling with my English. "I have pictures, though."

Mr. Tim held a strange twinkle in his eye. "Bring the pictures tomorrow."

"Okay," I said, confused.

The next time I saw Mr. Tim, I gave him the few pictures of myself that I could find.

"Great," he said. "I'll give these to my friends and see if anyone needs a contortion act."

My heart leapt. I couldn't believe it. Mr. Tim was going to help me out.

In the weeks to come, I trained hard on my solo act, wanting to make myself stronger in the event that a new audition should turn up as a result of Mr. Tim's inquiries. I prayed to Buddha every night, wanting desperately for things to work out.

The end of the tour was approaching, and everyone had begun talking about how they wanted to find a new contract. Everyone was nervous about whether they would be retained with Ringling or sent back home.

Almost two months after I first spoke to Mr. Tim about my intentions, he came backstage with a group of people, everyone talking animatedly.

"Hi, Mr. Tim," I said, my heart racing.

"Hello, Akto," he said with a bright smile. "Hey, listen. After the show, come up to see me in the office."

I nodded, my heart racing. I spent the rest of the show terrified about what Mr. Tim might have to tell me. Finally, when the show was over, I went back to see him. When I walked into the office, he smiled.

"How are you?"

"Good, thank you," I said.

"Your English has really improved," he said proudly. "Keep learning."

I nodded.

He leaned forward at his desk. "Well, Akto, I have good news for you. A friend of mine wants to hire you into his next show. We're going to call him right now so you can speak to him."

I'd never felt more happy and frightened at the same time.

Mr. Tim called his friend and started talking to him. I'm not sure what they said because I was too worried about commanding my own English that I couldn't pay attention. Before I even knew what was happening, he handed the phone to me.

I said hello to the man on the other end of the line, but don't remember much of anything else. I nearly fainted, I was so nervous. I talked to the man briefly before handing the phone back to Mr. Tim.

"Well, Akto," Mr. Tim said after he hung up, "looks like you'll be performing for Tarzan Zerbini!"

I thanked Mr. Tim profusely. He told me that the show would not begin until March, and that it would take me into Canada for almost four months. "But this will keep you working. And you'll need a multiple visa so you can travel between Canada and the States. They'll pay you eight hundred and fifty dollars per week. Will that work for you?"

"Yes!" I said, leaping to my feet. "Even if it was less, I would take it." I wanted to hug Mr. Tim in that moment, but I restrained myself, thanking Mr. Tim over and over again.

When I stepped outside, I felt like I was riding a cloud. I thanked Buddha and my mother and father. I was so happy and relieved. I could now tell my siblings that I was staying in America and that I had a job.

—ดดด—

As it turned out, Mr. Tim managed to talk Tarzan Zerbini into taking me on not as a solo act, but as a duo, which was good because it meant that I could bring along my friend and fellow contortionist, Urnaa. She would help me make the hard adjustment to life alone in the States, and the two of us would provide company and support for one another while on the road. It meant taking less money—$750 each—but I didn't mind. It was better to know that I would have steady friendship than steady money.

I learned quickly that success in America requires hard work. Urnaa and I went to work early and often on our new contortion act. With our new contract in place, we were able to tell our Mongolian contact that we would be staying in America. Where I expected resistance from the lady who had watched over us for two years, what I got was her congratulations. She even offered to take a letter back to my family for me.

The last night with the Ringling circus was emotional for us all. We put on the performance of a lifetime and then we partied all night. Saying goodbye to the friends I had made over those two fateful years was one of the most difficult things I have ever had to do.

CHAPTER 20

The morning after I finished up my tour with Ringling, Urnaa and I got on a bus to the airport with Mr. Tim. Together we flew to Washington DC, where Mr. Tim would put us up in his extra apartment for the three months until our next contract began. Mr. Tim went on to Florida, where he had his offices, leaving us behind to take in the capital on our own.

For the first few days, Urnaa and I just laid around in the apartment, watching TV and occasionally calling home. After two years of nonstop work, we figured we had earned it. But it wasn't long until we got terribly bored. We broke the television because we didn't know how to properly use the remote. And we broke the microwave because we weren't aware you couldn't load it up with something wrapped in aluminum foil. Just before we were to leave, we broke the stove and managed to lock ourselves out of the apartment, as well.

We were so nervous about the damage, fearing what Mr. Tim might say when he realized we had broken his appliances. But we finally worked up the courage to ask the superintendent of the building for help, and he took care of everything.

When we confessed to Mr. Tim over the phone later that night, he just laughed, saying that everything was fine. He even waived the $800 phone bill we unknowingly rang up in calling Mongolia so many times.

———

The middle of February finally arrived. We met the new performers and our new director. We were introduced then to our trailer and a man who would drive us around while we were on tour. We liked both of them, the trailer being spacious and the driver being quite a character.

With our new circus, we did many shows in Canada. We would have one or two days off between each show, depending on how far we had to travel to reach the next town. Mr. Tim came to visit us in Canada many times, having taken us under his wing as he did.

The last month before the end of our tour with the new circus, we were asked if we wanted to come back for the next season. We told our boss that we would think about it, preferring instead to travel to Chicago to see if we could find work there. We learned quickly that Chicago is big on Broadway shows, movies, and the commercial industry, but not much on circus acts. But we did learn during our time there that Las Vegas was the place to take our particular talents.

Without knowing anything about how to make it in America, I still felt compelled to follow my dreams. I was a single girl with two suitcases full of clothes and nothing else. Urnaa decided that she too would travel to Las Vegas to search for work. So we passed up our contract offer with Tarzan and called our agent, a man named Mr. Tibor Alexander, asking him if he could find us work in Vegas.

"I'll contact a woman I know down there," Tibor said. "She used to work for me. I'll see if she can help."

A few days later, we got a call back from Tibor telling us that his friend could put us up in a decent house for low rent. So we both bought one-way plane tickets to Vegas and geared ourselves up to start our new and glamorous lives.

Little did I know that this would be the beginning of a new and dark time for me.

—◦◦◦—

It was the beginning of September in 1994 when we landed in Las Vegas. As it turned out, we would be renting a house from this lady who lived with her boyfriend. In any case, she put us up in a small bedroom that we had to share. It was good enough for us while we looked around for work.

Urnaa and I spent the first week in Vegas taking the bus around town, trying to talk to as many agents and producers as we could. We would often miss our bus, which meant we would have to wait in the hot sun for an hour, as the Las Vegas bus system was pretty poor at the time.

The money grew short far quicker than we ever would have thought possible. During our first three years in America, we were on tour, so all we ever had to pay for was food and entertainment. But now we had rent, phone bills, electric bills, and any number of other expenses to account for. The going was difficult, and soon we had little money at all.

Times grew desperate. Urnaa and I began essentially begging for work, but to no avail. There just didn't seem to be any openings in Las Vegas for a pair of Mongolian contortionists. There came a time when I nearly gave up hope.

One day, I was looking through my notebook when I found a phone number for a friend of ours who had worked with us at Ringling: a juggler. My heart leapt as I remembered that he had told us that he planned to move to Vegas after our tour with Ringling.

I picked up the phone and called the number. Immediately, a man answered.

"May I speak to Joel?" I said.

"He's in the shower," the man replied. "If you'll leave your number, I'll let him know you called."

I left my number with the man, and half an hour later, Joel called back. "Otgo!" he bellowed into the line.

"Joel!" I said, smiling for the first time in what felt like weeks. "Urnaa and I have moved to Vegas."

"No kidding! We should get together. I'd love to introduce you to my girlfriend. She's visiting from Japan."

"That sounds great!" I said, and we made plans to meet at Joel's sister's party a couple of days later.

It might not have been a work contact, but as low as Urnaa and I were feeling, it was good to have something like a meeting with an old friend to look forward to.

When the day of the party came, a problem presented itself: we didn't have any transportation. So I called Joel and asked if he knew how we could get a ride to his sister's house. Joel said that he couldn't pick us up himself, as he drove a motorcycle, but that he could send his friend, Andy, to pick us up in his car.

"If you can just get to MGM, Andy will pick us all up, and we'll go."

I agreed that it sounded like a good plan. I then went to fetch Urnaa, get dressed, and head to the bus stop.

Later that afternoon, we all stood in the MGM parking lot. Joel introduced us to his roommate, Andy.

"Hello," Andy said. "Nice to meet you."

I might have been attracted to the handsome young man if I hadn't been so preoccupied about how to find work.

At the party, we were delighted to find that many of the people we had known from Ringling were in attendance. It was such a nice time meeting up with everyone again.

"You know," Urnaa said, elbowing me playfully, "Joel's roommate keeps following you everywhere. I think he likes you."

"What?" I said incredulously. "He is *not* following me. You're crazy."

Urnaa laughed. "Just pay attention, Otgo. He's everywhere you turn."

Of course the moment Urnaa left, Andy came over to talk to me—only proving her point. I didn't want to be rude, so I talked to him, but in truth, I didn't want to get into any kind of relationship while I was still trying to make it in Vegas. We made small talk, but my heart was never really in it.

When the party was over, Joel told us they were going to take us back to our house. And when we arrived at our home, we thanked everybody and said good night.

"Maybe we all should have dinner again soon," Joel said, looking sidelong at Andy.

"Sounds good," I said, and we left it at that.

Three days later, Joel called us, saying that he and Andy wanted to invite us to dinner at their house that weekend. Had Urnaa and I not been so bored, we might have refused. But as the fates would have it, we were terribly bored.

Saturday arrived, and Joel came over to pick us up. When we walked in the house, we found Andy cooking. He welcomed us in and said he was happy we could come over. As Andy prepared the food, we all enjoyed a few drinks, and everybody went outside to smoke. Through the window, I saw that Andy was busy cooking and was all alone. So I excused myself and went inside to ask if he needed any help.

He smiled. "You can clean some garlic for me."

I cleaned the garlic, and we started talking. He seemed like a pretty nice guy. He cooked spaghetti and meatballs as we spoke, and it turned out to be delicious.

We had a great deal of fun that night, and even more to drink. We wound up having to sleep over because everyone was too drunk to drive. Andy put Urnaa and me up in the extra bedroom and then left us alone for the night.

The next morning, we went to IHOP for breakfast. After breakfast, Andy drove us home, and as he lingered outside our doorway, his engine idling, he asked me if he could call me sometime.

"Okay," I said, feeling my cheeks warm.

From that day onward, Andy would call me often. I kept busy with looking for work, sending video and pictures to every game in town, but I always made time for Andy's calls. It was the only thing in my life that didn't bring me stress.

—⟨ℕ⟩—

Urnaa and I had to work hard to stretch what little money we had left. We always paid our rent first, so at least we would have a place to stay, but we often fell behind on the phone bills.

Andy would ask me out on dates all the time, and I would usually refuse because I didn't have any money to spend. But eventually, he insisted that we go out. He took me to a movie called *Legends of the Fall*.

We were left to eat the meager groceries that Urnaa and I could afford. We would eat a concoction of hamburger meat, flour, and onions called "lazy dumplings" quite often. In time, we ran so low on money that Urnaa had to leave the apartment and go live with her boyfriend, who was still working with Ringling.

These were dire times, but I refused to give up. I could have called Mr. Tim, I supposed, but I didn't want to ask for any more handouts. I just knew that I could survive on my own.

After Urnaa left, I was scared all the time. All I could do was pray to God and to my parents. I ran out of money and didn't have any work. The only food I had was a little bit of sourdough, and I stretched that out for two full weeks. The hunger I felt is difficult to describe.

One day, I went out to a casino in search for work, and when I returned, my roommate told me I had three days to get out of the house.

Now I was hungry, broke, unemployed, and homeless. I spent the last three nights in my apartment crying, unable to sleep. But then, on the third day, I noticed the sun rising outside my window, and with it came a new hope. I sat up in bed, telling myself that I just needed to pray.

I wrenched open the curtain, revealing the morning sun in all its glory. I got down on my knees and began to pray for strength in these difficult times. When I finished, I felt much calmer. And just as I finally managed to doze off to sleep, the phone rang. It was Andy.

"Can I take you out for dinner tonight?" he asked me.

I was starving, so I readily agreed.

"Great! I'll pick you up at five."

By five, I had cleaned myself up and packed my few things, telling my landlady that I would move out after dinner. I saw Andy's car pull up in front of the house, so I crept past the glares of my former roommate and my landlady and made my way out to Andy's car. Andy got out and opened my door for me, which I found particularly chivalrous, given the way I felt in that moment.

We went to a restaurant called the Draft House, where Andy quickly got to work worrying about whether I liked his choice. I didn't care what kind of restaurant we were in because I just wanted to eat some food.

We had beers with our steaks and potatoes, and I ate and drank ravenously, hardly speaking a word to Andy. When I finished, I finally looked up at him to thank him for this wonderful meal, and I saw that he had hardly touched his food and was looking at me rather bemused. I felt so embarrassed that I couldn't speak.

"Are you okay?" he asked after a time.

I lost it. As much as I wanted to hold back my tears, I couldn't stop myself. Crying and making a scene, I told Andy about everything that had happened to me over the past month, about how I was broke and now homeless.

A few times during my scene, the waitress came over to check on us, but turned immediately away when she noticed that I was bawling. My embarrassment deepened, but there was something about sharing my feelings with Andy that made me feel better.

"It sounds to me like your landlady just wanted you out for no reason," Andy offered.

I nodded, feeling immensely better knowing that at least one person on the planet believed me.

"You know," he said, sounding hesitant, "if you want, you can stay in my house. I have the extra bedroom. The guy who usually stays there won't be back for another six months. I won't need any rent money or anything. No pressure, either. It's totally up to you."

As kind as the offer was, I still couldn't get past the idea that Andy was somehow trying to take advantage of me. I had been so used to people doing just that by that time in my life that I just couldn't trust anyone. Gratefully, I told him I would think about it.

After dinner, he asked me if I was okay to go home by myself, and I told him I would be fine.

"If there is any problem," he said as he was dropping me off, "or if your landlady bothers you again, you can call me and I'll come get you. Okay?"

I nodded, crying again.

That night, having bartered for one more evening to get myself together, I thought for a long while about Andy's offer. On the one hand, I wasn't sure if I could trust him. On the other, I had nowhere else to go. Truly, I was torn.

The next morning, the landlady was waiting outside my door to throw me out. Suitcases in hand, I made the decision to contact Andy.

Living with Andy would turn out to be the best thing I ever did. He was always a gentleman, making sure that he wasn't taking advantage of my dire situation. But with his honesty and chivalry, it was difficult for me not to fall completely in love with him—which I did, quickly and hard.

"I just want you to know, Otgo," he would always say, "that you're safe here. Don't be scared or nervous about living with me. You will never have to worry about me."

In one remarkable day, my life changed for the better. With Andy's help, I was delivered from the darkness and set down in the light. This would be my new beginning.

CHAPTER 21

Finally, in early spring, I got a call about a show in Maine, of all places. I called Urnaa, and we got our act back together. We would be in Maine for two weeks, and that would lead to other jobs here and there. Before I knew it, we had been traveling and working for five and a half months.

Everything was going great. Whenever I didn't have work, I would take classes to become a bartender and cocktail waitress. When I got my certificate, I wanted to go to work at a nice lounge downtown, but I found that I couldn't be hired because my visa was for a performer, not a bartender.

I also discovered that since I hadn't worked for six months prior to my job in Maine, I had to leave the States for six months before returning. This was a particularly difficult blow to take, because I hadn't achieved my dream yet. I thought about going back to Canada to work for a while, but in the end, none of that really seemed possible anymore. I was in love with Andy, and I just couldn't imagine leaving him for half a year.

One day, Andy came home after his second job.

"Will you marry me?" he asked—just like that.

I was shocked. Completely taken aback. We hadn't spoken of marriage before this moment. In fact, I had never even thought about it. But at the same time, I knew I loved him very much, so I quickly said yes.

Andy had never looked happier. "Okay then!" He clapped his hands together once, beaming. "We'll get married soon!"

"Soon?" I said. "What's your hurry?"

"We'll do it in a week!"

"A week?" I could hardly believe what I was hearing. "But what about my visa and my having to leave, and we'll have to plan the wedding and—"

"Don't you worry," Andy interrupted. "I will take care of everything."

Indeed, Andy remained true to his promise to take care of everything. All I had to do was rent a wedding dress, and everything else was set up for me.

On the day of the wedding, I asked Urnaa and my friend from Ringling, Goulia, to stand up for me. Since I had nobody to walk me down the aisle, I called Mr. Tim Holst. He readily agreed to do the honor, and that made me feel good.

On July 17, 1995—which also happened to be my birthday—at a small church called the Little Chapel of the West, I married the love of my life, my dearest Andy.

Mr. Tim arrived that morning and came directly to the church. He walked me down the aisle and handed me to Andy.

"Please take care of her," he whispered.

Andy nodded proudly.

After the ceremony, we had a small party with our family and friends. It was a simple affair, but everyone seemed to have a great time.

Almost fourteen months after Urnaa and I first moved to Vegas, we got our first break. The Excalibur Hotel Casino was looking for a "strolling entertainer," which meant we would have to do three shows per day. Between each show, we were required to walk around the casino floor, talking to guests. We were to make $650 per week for five working days and two days off.

Things took off from there. Right after we began at Excalibur, Ed Finley called to tell us that we had been hired to perform at a number of halftime shows for the NBA, the NHL, and a few NCAA basketball games. I couldn't believe our luck. To perform for such large events was quite an honor.

But when we learned how much we would be paid, it bowled us over entirely.

"They're offering to pay you $2,300 each for every show you do," Ed Finley said.

It was difficult to fathom that kind of money after living so long in poverty.

By late 1995, we were working for almost all the teams in the NBA. We went to Chicago, Orlando, Salt Lake City, Phoenix, Washington, Miami, Los Angeles, Toronto, Houston—just about everywhere the NBA was played. We did shows for a number of NHL and NCAA teams as well. It was a whirlwind of work and activity, and yet it afforded me plenty of time with Andy. I loved everything about it.

Through the year 2000, we worked for many different companies, including many famous theaters and shows, such as *The Tonight Show with Jay Leno*. Our act took us all over the United States and Europe.

Sometime into one of our latest tours, I began to get sick. Every day, I would vomit, and I couldn't figure it out, because it didn't feel like the flu. As a constant traveler, I was used to getting the flu, and this just wasn't it. I was always tired and always moody.

One night, I had a dream about my mother. This took me by surprise, as it was the first time I had dreamed about my mother in quite some time. She smiled at me, taking me into her arms.

"Why do I feel this way?" I asked her.

"You are not alone," she said.

And before I could ask her what she meant, she smiled and was gone.

When I woke, I felt sad, as if my mother had somehow left me. But a few weeks later, when I went to see the doctor, I discovered what she had meant. She wasn't leaving me; I was being joined.

"You're going to be a mother!" the doctor said.

I just started crying.

"Are you okay?" the doctor asked.

"Yes!" I cried. "Yes, I'm just happy, is all." I couldn't stop crying because I realized then why my mother told me that I wasn't going to be alone anymore.

"Well, take your time," the doctor said. "You can sit here as long as you need." He then went to fetch me a glass of water and handed me a little book about babies and motherhood.

That night, when I told Andy, he was giddy. He called his parents, bursting with pride.

I had discovered that I was two months pregnant, but I still had contracts to honor—so I did just that until it became too difficult to continue. By the time Urnaa and I reached the height of our fame—when we had our pictures taken to appear in *Sports Illustrated*—I was four months pregnant and ready to retire.

God would continue to smile on me even after I became too pregnant to perform. As it turned out, four Mongolian contortionists and their coach had been invited to Las Vegas to perform in a new Cirque du Soleil show called *O*. And given that they struggled with English and the new culture, I offered to help them out because I knew how hard it was to start from the beginning without any assistance. I spent much of the rest of my pregnancy ushering the girls around, laughing with them, and helping them learn the ways of the new world.

From the doctor, I knew that Andy and I were to have a baby girl, so I would often talk to the Mongolian girls about a good Mongolian name for my daughter. I wanted to give her an American first name—Andy and I had decided on Emily—and a Mongolian middle name. In time, the girls came up with Od, which we all thought was particularly meaningful, since it meant "Star" in Mongolian.

In the middle of September, my baby girl, Emily Od Waller, arrived. Once she was delivered, and I was allowed to hold her for the first time, I couldn't stop crying. I was so happy. This was truly the happiest moment of my life, looking down at my little girl, with my wonderful husband leaning over us. She would be my world for as long as I lived.

AFTERWORD

When I think about my life as one unit, my mind keeps going back to the concept of motherhood. For as prophetic as my birth story came to be, I can't help but believe that greater things are ahead for my little Emily. I was born into a humble home, an impoverished home, to parents who did everything they could to provide for us in the face of a harsh environment and a harsher government. Emily has been born into a much more comfortable setting. Andy and I are happy. We live in a wonderful home and in a country that is truly free. It is a cliché, certainly, but the sky is truly the limit for my daughter.

After a life of working hard, I am finally in a position where I can relax and let life come to me. Nobody told me how to be a mother, so that is my only remaining consistent struggle. But not to worry. I'm learning more about how to do this job every day.

One day, as I was playing with Emily, it struck me that she was such a beautiful and happy baby. And in her beauty and happiness, I finally found the peace I had been searching for my entire life. As I watched her bounce and giggle, I knew I had to let go of my past.

I made the decision right then and there that I would forgive everyone in my past who had done me harm. I would do my best to release the haunting memories of the men who molested me. I would try to let go of my insecurity over my body image. I would try to find peace with the fact that I was never able to say goodbye to my mother. For the first time, I knew it would be possible to forgive everyone and everything in my past who had done me harm. I could stop dwelling on my past. I could begin to heal.

The thing about pain—especially about deep-seated and longstanding pain of this nature—is that it never fully disappears. It's like a burn. The wound may heal in time, but the scar will always remain. Until that moment, my wound was still unhealed. But in that moment when I finally let go, I felt as if I had expelled a terrible thing from within myself—a dark creature that had been chewing me from the inside out. I was able then to tell Andy about the less glamorous parts of my past, of the things that had troubled me for so long. I had held these stories back from him early on in our relationship because I truly believed he would leave me if he knew how damaged I was.

But the truth is that I wasn't damaged. I have lived a sometimes difficult life, to be certain, but everything happened to me for a reason. I have become a better woman for it, and a better wife and mother. And on those days when tears return to me, I have a wonderful husband to hug me and tell me that everything will be all right.

"You're so beautiful," he often says, and no matter how many times he says it, I still swoon.

For the longest time, I never thought I was beautiful. It was a difficult thing to imagine, given that I had always been called fat and ugly as a young child. When I came to America, people began using this new term on me: beautiful. I used to plug up my ears and wonder why everyone always had to make fun of me. I just couldn't believe that I was beautiful. But now I have a husband who tells me this every day. It has helped me to let go of the darkness I had always held for myself, helped me to see things in a different light.

There is a saying in America: "Just be yourself." I heard it for the first time one day while I was watching TV. For someone who is born free, it's a simple phrase, one that might seem even a little naïve. But for someone who was born in a country like Socialist Mongolia, the concept of just being oneself is overwhelming. Until the day I finally let go of all my horrors, I was never truly myself. As a child oppressed by her government and shaped into a contortionist by hardline coaches and trainers, I had no choice but to be who everyone else wanted me to be. I had no choice but to be perfect. To be anything less would have been considered failure.

This is not to say that I regret my choices in life. I have always known that God gave me a special gift. I have had this natural talent to perform and bend myself since I was a little girl. No one pushed me into this. And now that I have made it in this profession, I know that I wouldn't have done things any other way.

These days, my smiles are real. I don't worry about pleasing others quite like I used to. I am free.

The first time I noticed this change in me was when I was next on stage. Contortionism has many different traditions. This is owed perhaps to the fact that many countries—Mongolia, Russia, Germany, the United States, and many countries in Eastern Europe being chief among them—have contributed their own unique influences to the art. Some performers act with great speed, others with almost robotic precision. Still others take a jerky, freakish approach. All forms are acceptable and effective representations of the art, but I have always believed—and most in the world of contortionism would agree with me—that the graceful Mongolians have always done it best. So I have always attempted to perform with as much grace as possible. But until that next time I took the stage, my grace always had to be forced. Now, much more than before, my performance was passionate, more alive than it had ever been. I didn't have to fake my intensity or my happiness to be in the limelight. It just came naturally. I had finally come out of the box.

I am no longer ashamed of myself. I no longer blame myself for my mother's death. I have stopped trying to please everyone else before tending to my own needs. I no longer worry what people think about me. I have stopped trying to pretend to be someone else. I have begun to love myself and accept myself for who I am.

The result is that I am able to give more than ever before. I have begun giving to others in the form of teaching. I provide lessons to aspiring contortionists and also teach classes on flexibility (I like to communicate the point that flexibility is healthy, no matter how old you are). More important, I have begun giving to God. I do believe in God. I believe in something greater than me. And I believe that even though we all have different forms of belief—from Catholics to Buddhists to Muslims to Mormons, and everything between—those who truly believe have equal access to the path toward happiness and peace. God has led me here. He has blessed me with my family, my friends, my new home in America, my ability as a contortionist, and my newfound willingness to give of myself. I am so grateful.

My family and I moved to Chicago in October of 2000. There, Andy, Emily, and I became students under Dr. Natsagdorj, our spiritual teacher. We would return to Las Vegas in 2004, when Andy lost his mother, but we would take our faith with us.

With my newfound happiness, success, and faith, I decided that it was time to finally fulfill my promise to myself. So on June 29, 2002, Emily and I traveled to Mongolia. It was eleven years from when I first set out for America.

It is amazing how much Mongolia has changed in just over a decade. I hardly recognized the city in which I grew up. My friends and family had trouble recognizing me as well, saying that I had changed a great deal.

I have changed a great deal because I wanted to change. But at the same time, I will never forget where I came from and who I am. This book represents that effort to remember. It has been a struggle for me to write, as English is certainly not my first language. And beyond that, it has often been trying to conjure up troubling memories from my past. But as I write this, it occurs to me that I have completed my difficult task.

I am grateful to my wonderful husband, Andy, to our spiritual guidance teacher, Natsagdorj, and to my dear friend and mentor, Mr. Tim Holst. Whenever I need advice, whether social, spiritual, or professional, I can always trust them to help me.

Upon returning to Las Vegas, I joined up with a large performing troupe. At one particular show, Mr. Tim traveled in to watch me perform. After the show, he asked me to join him for dinner. At the restaurant, he placed his hand over mine.

"Otgo," he said, "did I ever tell you why I helped you stay in America?"

"No," I said, my eyes widening. "Why?"

Mr. Tim gave a little smile. "Because you were the only foreign performer who was ever honest with me when I asked you if you planned to return home."

I laughed, realizing then how much my life hinged on one simple decision: to tell the truth, as my mother had taught me, and to face my own destiny.

"You changed my life forever, Mr. Tim," I told him with teary eyes. "Without you, none of this would have been possible."

I must thank Mr. Tim Holst from the bottom of my heart. I must thank my dear husband for everything he has done for me. And I must thank my parents, who brought me into this world. They gave me my life; the rest of it was totally up to me. I still think about those clouds. I still wonder where they have been, where they are going, and who they might inspire after me. And, yes, like those clouds and those who view them, I have endured a great deal—so much good and so much bad—but in the end, what I have found is love. Love has helped heal my wounds.

Printed in the United States
By Bookmasters